The American Absurd

Pynchon, Vonnegut, and Barth

by

Robert A. Hipkiss

NATIONAL UNIVERSITY PUBLICATIONS
ASSOCIATED FACULTY PRESS, INC.
Port Washington, N.Y. • New York City • London

Associated Faculty Press, Inc.
National University Publications
Series in Modern and Contemporary Literature

Advisory Editor
Dr. Linda W. Wagner

Jeffrey, *A Grit's Triumph*
Hipkiss, *The American Absurd*
Holden, *Landscapes of the Self*
Rahming, *The Evaluation of the West Indian's*
        Image in the Afro-American Novel

Manufactured in the United States of America

Published by
Associated Faculty Press, Inc.
Port Washington, N.Y.

Library of Congress Cataloging in Publication Data

Hipkiss, Robert A., 1935-
   The American absurd.

   (Series in modern and contemporary literature)
(National university publications)
   Includes bibliographical references and index.
   1. American fiction—20th century—History and criticism. 2. Absurd
(Philosophy) in literature. 3. Existentialism in literature. 4. Pynchon,
Thomas—Philosophy. 5. Vonnegut, Kurt—Philosophy. 6. Barth,
John—Philosophy. I. Title. II. Series.
PS374.A28H56   1984   813'.54'09   83-22306
ISBN 0-8046-9340-4

Contents

About the Author

Robert A. Hipkiss received a Bachelor of Arts degree from San Jose State College, and Master of Arts and Doctor of Philosophy degrees from the University of California in Los Angeles. He is the author of a prior book *Jack Kerouac, Prophet of the New Romanticism* published by Kansas University Press in 1976. Presently Dr. Hipkiss is a Professor of English at California State University at Long Beach.

Preface

In teaching various courses in American twentieth-century literature, the author has found that students find themselves struggling to comprehend a form of literature that bears little resemblance to what has come before when they study the post-World War II literature of the Absurd, whether it be John Barth's "Lost in the Funhouse" in a short story course, or a work such as Kurt Vonnegut's *Slaughterhouse Five* in the study of the American novel. A knowledge of the traditional criteria and methodology of the story and novel just does not help much to elicit the meaning of these works.

It became apparent that what was needed was an introduction to this specialized genre that would delineate the central themes and character conflicts, examine the key symbols, explain their various methods and techniques, and, together, provide the reader with an appreciation and understanding of the full dimensions of the American Absurd.

The introduction to this book explains my choice of authors for this work. Many critics have been consulted, but in order to keep the focus on the works under review, I have limited my discussion of other scholars' critical views to the ones I found most incisive and most pertinent, although generalized critical appraisals have been acknowledged.

A basic understanding of each author's thought and technique in their major works has been sought without belaboring material that has already been too heavily mined by the critics.

Introduction

The Nature of Absurdity and its Literary Manifestations

The absurd is at base a very serious view of life. It is a view of man as a being who must strive to attain goals that provide only temporary satisfaction and that have no meaning beyond themselves. Like Sisyphus, legendary king of Corinth in ancient Greece, man is condemned to roll a stone uphill, only to have it roll back down again, and to have to return to the foot of the hill to roll it back up once more. According to Albert Camus, the French Existentialist, the only triumph Sisyphus can know is when he is walking back down the hill; it is the triumph of scorn for the stupidity of his predicament as well as the acceptance of the rock as "his thing."[1] There is no escape, just the recognition of what the situation factually is, without recourse to the illusions of hope that are the traditional palliatives of religious and secular ideologies.

The Absurdist regards the human condition as one in which man is caught between the extremes of birth and death, phenomena which he cannot possibly hope to understand. For him there is neither ontology nor eschatology. Man's consciousness is, simply *is*.

To dramatize the disjunction between man's ideal conceptualizations and his mortal condition, the artist of the Absurd carries the ideal and its factual inapplicability to an extreme. The result is farce, surrealism, and a violent collapse of the character and his illusory world. This is the course of events in the French Theater of the Absurd in the plays of Eugene Ionesco and Samuel Beckett, and in the contemporary German drama of Friedrich Durrenmatt. The exaggerations of dialogue, action, and scene create symbolic leitmotifs on the appearance-reality theme that engage and puzzle the minds of the audience. The Absurd is nothing if not intellectual art.

The impossibility of human freedom has occupied many of the writers of the Absurd in Europe. Beckett's illustration of man's bondage to his momentary

1

"betters" in the Pozzo and Lucky partnership in *Waiting for Godot,* and the bondage of men passing time in the prison of their hopes and beliefs in the eternal waiting of Vladimir and Estragon in the same drama are cardinal metaphors of the Absurd.

The tenuousness of personal identity in a modern world in which classes upset one another, where there is great population mobility, and where all authority is suspect, is also a strong theme in the European works. Arthur Adamov's *Professor Taranne* and *Tous Contre Nous* are illustrative, the former showing the loss of identity of a professional man who is suddenly the victim of slander and discrimination, and the latter more candidly showing the cruelty of anti-Semitism. Eugene Ionesco is, of course, the premier dramatist of man's empty self. In *The Bald Soprano, The Chairs, The Lesson,* and others of his plays he shows how we depend upon material objects, our possessions, for our identity, how easily reputations are made and destroyed, and how little we really know about ourselves and others. The characters' attachment to the trappings of respectability, their pompous, nonsensical speeches that do not communicate, all suggest individual isolation and a reliance on the thinnest of appearances to cover the abyss of the unknown life and the unknown self.

In American literature the Absurd has been with us since the publication of Mark Twain's *The Mysterious Stranger* (1916), in which the self is described as a "vagrant thought, a useless thought, a homeless thought, wandering forlorn among the empty eternities."[2] In that work Satan gives Theodore, his boy initiate, two weapons against the absurdity of a solipsistic universe, the weapon of Sisyphus, intellectual laughter, and the weapon of the Cartesian idealist, the capacity to "dream better dreams," to create more satisfying illusions than those offered by conventional religion.

To Existentialists who follow Twain in American letters, such as Ernest Hemingway and Wallace Stevens, although life is cosmically absurd they still believe that man can struggle against absurdity, by living with intensity, by being true to his own moral code, and by fulfilling the demands of his chosen profession. If there is no life after death, these writers take comfort in the belief that nature will endure and that their lives and work are, if done with personal integrity, a meaningful contribution to the life of their era.

To the American post-World War II Absurdists, man is not able to meaningfully direct his own affairs. Like the American and European Existentialists, the Absurdists preserve the Judeo-Christian ethics as an ideal, but they see man as inevitably corrupted by his drive for power. Morality is narrowly self-centered and man's choices are selfish and heavily rationalized. The Absurdists see man's institutions as corrupt, as do the Existentialists, but the Absurdists also find man's freedom very limited, his attempts at opposing a personal code to the absurdity of existence doomed to failure, and personal heroism impossible except in acts of moral refusal and in the fragile fantasies of the tortured mind. More often than the Existentialists they have to settle for momentary escape, stoic endurance, and basic human sympathy in place of more ideal, stalwart values. The Absurdists have less faith in human progress and tend to see history as repetitive. They see man's instinctive drives as responsible for forming his intellectual rationalizations, his free choice as largely illusion, and his educability very much in question. The Existentialist believes that man can learn from experience and create a meaningful life for himself, but the Absurdist finds life's experiences so contradictory and unresolvable that he can only admit to confusion and express the need for a nonrational means of knowing. Existentialist humor is stoic; the Absurdist's is black. The former has tragic possibilities: the victim of the joke is noble and his suffering commendable. Black humor verges on despair: the victim is not noble but holding on, grim and pathetic but determined. I-thou love is possible and ennobling for the Existentialist; it is cruel/kind, an expression of man's drive to power and possession for the Absurdist. The Absurdist substitutes sympathy and decency for love as the beneficent values of human cohesion.

Books have been written by various American authors that exemplify one or more traits of the Absurd. The author of this study has selected three authors whose works as a whole represent the dimensions of the Absurd most completely (authors who have written as Americans out of the American experience), in an attempt to discover and illustrate not only the dimensions of the Absurd generally, but to show how historical American literary themes are treated in this genre. It is for this reason that Vladimir Nabokov is not treated except in relation to the works of those authors included in this volume. Nor has the author treated the work of that other exile Jerzy Kosinski, whose novels such as *Painted Bird, Being There,* and *The Devil Tree* might otherwise qualify for consideration.

An author such as James Purdy, whose works range from standard realism in *The Nephew* to absurd quest in *Malcolm* and *Cabot Wright Begins,* though a qualified practitioner, writes in and out of the genre and tends to concentrate on the lamentable failure of love, one of the reasons why this author characterized him in an earlier work as a "new romanticist."[3]

Another author with a sizable output who might qualify for a study of the Absurd is John Hawkes. Like Nabokov, his characters parody their own self-pretentions in a manner that suggests the ineradicably illusory quality of life. Hawkes' *Travesty* is, moreover, a fine parodic put-down of existential heroism in an absurd universe. For a study of the gripe of human compulsion and the failure of intellectual formulation, Nabokov and Hawkes offer exemplary works in *Lolita, Pale Fire, Second Skin,* and *Travesty,* among others. Hawkes, though, like his Russian-born contemporary does not deal, for the most part, with identifiably American themes and only vaguely with American experience.

Perhaps the most obvious omission is Joseph Heller. *Catch-22* was his chief absurd novel, and yet its ending is more existential and romantic than absurd. In subsequent works, though the social conventions of business and government are treated as absurd, the protagonist is shown to be less a victim of an absurd world than of his immaturity. His salvation is found, weakly, in *Something Happened* and, strongly, in *Good as Gold* in old-fashioned family responsibility. Moreover, since Heller's *Catch-22* has been the most heavily criticized of all the American Absurd novels, most readers are already sufficiently familiar with this book.

Other authors' works come to mind as representative of the genre: Jack Kerouac's *On the Road*, Richard Brautigan's *Trout Fishing in America*, Robert Coover's *The Universal Baseball Association, Inc., J. Henry Waugh, Prop.*, Ishmael Reed's *Flight to Canada*, John Irving's *The World According to Garp*, and Tom Robbins's *Even Cowgirls Get the Blues*. None of these authors has the *oeuvre* in the genre, however, that this study requires. One also thinks of the plays of Edward Albee, deeply indebted as they are to the French Theater of the Absurd, but the chief literary mode in American literature remains the novel, and it seems best to concentrate this study upon this more developed form of literary expression.

The first author chosen for this study is Thomas Pynchon, whose *V.*, first copyrighted in 1961, is a keystone novel in linking considerations of the Absurd with the American literary traditon and whose *Gravity's Rainbow* may well be the capital of that artistic construction. The second author considered is Kurt Vonnegut, whose terse address to the basic philosophical questions of human existence in the guise of fantasy and ironic humor entitle him to more serious critical consideration than he has generally been accorded. John Barth, whose works are the last ones to be considered in this study, has created the largest *oeuvre* of them all and explores in greatest depth the role of the artist in the Absurd.

All of these authors experiment with forms of communication—cartoons, lyrics, jokes, narratives, metaphors, and signs. Two of them, Pynchon and Barth, are often described as Post-Modernists, and critics have dealth with them often in terms of their various modes of presentation to the exclusion of the thought behind their writing. The author of this work is not a Post-Modernist and is opposed to a strictly Structuralist approach to literature. Even those authors who have imbibed heavily the waters of Structuralism had to begin with a view of the world that is essentially historical and sociological in order to arrive at their reductive mode of expression or criticism. Moreover, it is still the critic's job to discover how truthful and valuable a work is to the general human concerns of mankind. And even the most nihilistic of authors can give us great insight into our position in the universe and help us establish ourselves on firmer ground in comprehension and expectation without destroying all hope of human betterment.

The three authors chosen well illustrate the central thesis of this study, that the American Absurdists, while showing the influence of the European Existential and Absurd writers, are essentially reevaluating the venerated nineteenth-century themes of American culture: (1) the assured destiny of a spiritually guided and, therefore, innately moral America; (2) the Americans as a new race, free of history's endless cycles of war and repression; (3) the reliability and inviolability of individual conscience and intuition; and (4) the ultimate necessity and triumph of self-reliance.

NOTES

1. Albert Camus, "The Myth of Sisyphus." In *Existentialism from Dostoevsky to Sartre,* edited by Walter Kaufman (New York: Meridian Books, 1957), pp. 312-15.
2. Mark Twain, "The Mysterious Stranger." In *Mark Twain's The Mysterious Stranger and the Critics,* edited by John S. Tuckey (Belmont, Calif.: Wadsworth Publishing Co., 1968), p. 74.
3. Robert Hipkiss, *Jack Kerouac, Prophet of the New Romanticism* (Lawrence, Kan.: The Regents Press of Kansas, 1976), pp. 105-9.

Part I

Thomas Pynchon

Chapter 1
The Transcendental Quest Through Three Novels

Chapter 2
Method in the Madness

Chapter 1
The Transcendental Quest Through Three Novels

Thomas Pynchon is nothing if not historical since his Puritan New England past is intimately bound to the social history of the nation. William Pynchon, a judge at the Salem witchcraft trials in 1692 and a character in Nathaniel Hawthorne's *House of the Seven Gables,* was his ancestor. As with other sensitive writers at the very core of the New England tradition—from Jonathan Edwards through Ralph Waldo Emerson, Henry Adams, and T.S. Eliot,[1] to Robert Lowell—Pynchon seeks the assurance of a spiritual transcendence in a world in which there is far more evidence of damnation. He shoulders the guilt of past generations, of our woeful, warring ancestors, and carries this burden of grief and guilt through the streets of Valletta, Malta, in *V.,* into San Narciso, southern California, in *The Crying of Lot 49,* and into the lawless "Zone" of *Gravity's Rainbow* in search of a sign. And we follow him, with difficulty, but follow nevertheless, because were he to find it, we, thirsty inhabitants of the Waste Land, would see it too.

In his first novel, *V.,* the quest takes the form of a son's search for an understanding of his father's life. Herbert Stencil relates his neurotic interpretations of his own adventures to his "psychodontist," Eigenvalue. His father's letters are concerned with the elusive V, woman in several guises. There is Victoria Wrenn, a failed nun, whose ivory comb carries the figures of five crucified soldiers—Victoria, a queen for whom an empire was built. Later we meet Melanie L'Heuremaudit, whose mirror reflection of herself is her lesbian lover V. She is a "fetish," a sex symbol in the costume of a dancer, who at fifteen, in 1913, lay with her father. She is narcissistic, sterile, twentieth-century woman. V. is also Veronica Manganese, who has a clockwork eye, as does Vera Meroving, the mistress of the engineer Kurt Mondaugen. Eventually, V. is discovered under the robes of the Bad Priest of Malta as a woman with artificial limbs as well as a clockwork eye.

Many readers have noted the mutation of the woman V. from innocence and faith through fleshly pleasures and self-worship into mechanistic disintegration. Historically, the time of her change is around the turn of the century, with the changes having been completed by the end of World War I. Stencil sees Victoria standing at the crossing of the Via Purgatorio and the Via Inferno in Florence along the river Arno, at one of many of Pynchon's symbolic crossroads, a point at which she will abandon her belief in her own powers of individual moral agency, what Pynchon refers to as "virtu," abandoning herself to the currents of the coming age, as the power of V. transforms itself from the forces of faith (Henry Adams's Virgin) to the forces of technology (the Dynamo). It is also an age of the fox (deviousness) replacing the age of the lion (courage and heart).[2]

Considering Melanie's lesbianism, Stencil thinks, "Let her be a lesbian; let her turn to a fetish; let her die: she was a beast of venery and he had no tears for her."[3] (The abandonment of the lecherous to their own sin, the disgusted condemnation of an age, was, in fact, prefigured in Pynchon's first published story, "Mortality and Mercy in Vienna," when the host of a Washington party of civilized degenerates leaves them to be annihilated by a crazed American Indian.) Stencil's puritanical either/or attitude toward human morality is sharply contrasted against that of the Maltese, Fausto Maijstral, who feels that V., as the woman dressed as the Bad Priest, sincerely repents her vice-ridden life. Fausto takes an intellectual, all-accepting view of the world. Stencil's moral idealism also contrasts with the unimaginative acceptance of the schlemiel's role on the part of his friend Benny Profane, and the crazed concern for the lowly on the part of Father Fairing, whose parish was a sewer and whose parishoners were rats (animals that share with pigs the status of surrogates for a lost humanity in Pynchon's fabulated theology).

V. manifests itself as women, but is also Vheissu, the legendary land of ever-changing kaleidoscopic colors, once glimpsed by the explorer Godolphin and haunting him ever-after. Vheissu becomes Tyrone Slothrop's rainbow in *Gravity's Rainbow,* representative of a spiritual transcendence. V. is also Von Trotha, who led the execution of the black tribe of Herreros in German Southwest Africa around 1900. Moreover, V. is not only Veronica Manganese but Veronica the sewer rat. For Benny Profane, V. is a string of green mercury vapor lamps "receding in an asymmetric V to the east where it's dark and there are no more bars," a use of green lights that is similar to that of F. Scott Fitzgerald's image at the end of *The Great Gatsby* where the light on the end of Daisy's dock, at East Egg, represents the "orgiastic future" that always recedes from us. The letter *V* attaches itself to many characters and things in the novel, all of which are emanations of the central current of history and human life, what Henri Bergson called the *élan vital.* V. is "venery" in the sense of the instinctive forces that compel love and hate, creation and self-aggrandizement. It is also venery in the sense of the hunt undertaken by Stencil and on a less elevated level by Benny Profane. It is what drives us and what we envision, and it is in the visions that it projects through our perceiving selves that it gives us keys (or signs) as to its meaning.

The quest for meaning continues in Pynchon's next work, *The Crying of Lot 49*. Oedipa Maas inherits Stencil's role as the seeker after a moral order underlying an apparently amoral, perhaps inherently immoral, world. Like Stencil, she sees man's destiny in either/or terms. There is either a real moral counterforce (the Trystero, a moral conspiracy of alternate message carriers using a muted post horn symbol) to which she relates the promise of America as a land of freedom and equality), or just America, a sad legacy of the Founding Fathers, the most obvious aspect of which is the thirst for possessions, wealth, power, and control of Pierce Inverarity, a business magnate.

Oedipa is disposed to be neurotic. In order to cope, she has learned to impose order on her world through the willfull exercise of her imagination on its discordant elements. In Mexico, looking at a painting by the Spanish exile Remedios Varo, she realizes that her life is really a tapestry woven out of the tower of her own ego and to be looked upon as her own world. Like Rapunzel, the imprisoned maiden of German folklore, she is a prisoner in her tower, and "what keeps her where she is is magic, anonymous and malignant, visited on her from outside and for no reason at all."[4] The prison of one's own ego can be overcome only by a counterforce that opposes the customary modes of perception, the counterforce symbolized in this novel by the muted post horn, as it apparently is in Varo's painting "Invocation."

Pynchon goes to elaborate lengths to give the post horn another symbolic genesis. It was the symbol of a private postal system, Thurn and Taxis,[5] that covered most of Europe by the middle of the nineteenth century. Pynchon opposes it with the Trystero. Pynchon has a great facility for discovering real names that have suggested meanings that fit into his crazy-quilt scheme of things; for instance, *Remedios Varo,* suggesting remedial truth, truth of the imagination. If one looks at *Thurn* as close to the German word for "tower" (*Thurm*) and *Taxis* as the root of such a word as "taxonomy," one finds him speaking of the tower of the ego, the imprisoned self, imprisoned by fear and dislike of the social order, a force opposed by the Trystero, or those who meet to ambush (or to love, as in lover's trysts). It becomes evident before long, that this novel, in many ways a typical production of the sixties, centers on the individual's desire for freedom, spontaneity, and love in conflict with the forces of institutional authority.

Oedipa's tower is also much like Stephen Daedalus's tower in the first chapter of *Ulysses,* a set of mind that she must abandon if she wants to understand the world. When she becomes executrix of the will of Pierce Inverarity, she sees it as her duty to find out as much as she can about his activities and "to project a life." Her investigation, haphazard as it is, carries her into the bizarre world of business gamesmanship and self-love. She becomes acquainted with the passion for glamour and self-promotion that is part of the San Narciso style of life.

Her investigations spur the search for a counterforce that will oppose the institutions of personal wealth, power, and show. Once again the search is for a sign. She finds reference to the Trystero in a Jacobean play, *The Courier's Tragedy,* directed by Randolph Driblette. Professor Emory Bortz tells her that he thinks the word is an insertion by some Puritan transcribers who intended it as a curse on the play, the word standing for the evil principle in their universe. He also tells her that "Puritans were utterly devoted, like literary critics, to the Word." She is also cautioned by the play's director not to expect to discover truth through the process of detection. He himself meets the Infinite by walking into the ocean to his death.[6] An analysis of signs, then, is a questionable way to proceed to a grasp of first principles, though it is Oedipa's way, and it is the exercise that Pynchon puts his protagonists and his readers through in all three of his novels. If the end result is in doubt, the quest and its urgency are nonetheless real, and that is the emphasis Pynchon makes here and in *V.*

In *Gravity's Rainbow* Pynchon gives Tyrone Slothrop, his exhausting protagonist, deep Puritan origins. Cleanth Siegel, one of Pynchon's critics, has pointed out that "William Slothrop was a real New England Pilgrim who arrived in the same fleet as Pynchon's own ancestor William in 1630."[7] The fictional Slothrop has an ancestor who was a minister in Puritan times and who raised pigs, symbols of the Preterite, the vast majority of the human race, those who are not of the elect. Tyrone Slothrop's ancestors were always conscious of the sky wherein dwells the imponderable God and felt they owed nature a death, these busy men and women of the earth. Tyrone, however, is afraid of death without the Word, without a Hereafter to believe in. For the spiritual predestination of his ancestors he tries to substitute an "operational paranoia," the idea of a missile with his name on it, as though he did have a destiny.[8] The wartime atmosphere of Europe in the early 1940s feeds his paranoia and makes possible his half-belief in a kind of order. Better negative order than no order at all, it seems.

The world of Chance that the statistician Roger Mexico so fatalistically accepts for a time is not for Slothrop. Slothrop wants to believe that there is some authority, some purpose, behind life's events that leads man to a meaningful spiritual destiny. His mental set throughout the novel is typified when he backs out of the enormous rococo game room at the Casino Hermann Goering, where games of chance were played by the lords of misrule of the Hitler years. As he departs, it is "as if half, his ventral half, were being struck by kingly radiance: retreating from yet facing the Presence feared and wanted."[9] Slothrop would like to believe in rightful authority the way the British did in Empire, but he realizes more and more that "They," those who are in authority in the world, have no respect for the likes of him. He begins to feel more and more part of a system "where only destinations are important, attention is to long-term statistics, not individuals: and where the House always does, of course, keep turning a profit. . . ."[10]

Slothrop's nemesis is Edward Pointsman, the Pavlovian, whose mania for an orderly world makes all humans, including Slothrop, fair game for his conditioning experiments. A great number of Slothrop's adventures take place under the influence of sodium amytol, administered by Pointsman's orders. The scenes in which Slothrop is hallucinating his adventures while lying in Pointsman's hospital and the scenes that take place outside it run into one another often without transition, suggesting that their degree of truth and their place in Slothrop's quest for an acceptable view of things is really one and the same. Reality in Pynchon is in the mind, in any case, and he tends to regard the division between physical, objective reality and pure imagination as an easily crossed, unrelieved "lowland."

The intellectually opposite position to Pointsman is occupied by the statistician Roger Mexico, who sees life largely in terms of chance and probabilities. Mexico plots the German rocket strikes on England and finds that they are forming a perfect Poisson distribution of random probability. When Pointsman suggests that wherever rockets have already fallen they must stand less of a chance of falling again, Mexico says that he is guilty of the Monte Carlo fallacy, that each rocket is at the whim of incalculable forces that guide it independently from all other rockets, that there is simply no predicability.[11]

Mexico's statistics makes him fatalistic. In his lovemaking with Jessica Swanlake he is indiscriminate as to where they do it because one place is as safe as another according to his view of probabilities. Jessica is not accepting of the laws of chance. Ultimately she leaves Mexico to return to her dull organization-man husband Jeremy. Mexico feels the war infecting their relationship but he does not know how to keep it away. He comes increasingly to feel that he is being victimized, and, because of what Pointsman is doing to Slothrop, he too revolts.

Pointsman and Jeremy represent the System, a "They System of anonymous authority, all the more pernicious because of people's unconscious acceptance of it as the very structure of their thinking. For Pointsman survival comes down to "knowing the System better than the other chap, and how to use it."[12] In his thinking, there is no question of order, only of how well one understands and uses it. Pointsman is a dreadful creature of intellect without normal human compassion, and without a scientist's proper humility before the unknown. When he finds out that Slothrop's map of his sexual conquests is remarkably predictive of V-2 rocket strikes in and around London, he immediately seeks the cause. In his thinking there is no mere coincidence, and any means to the end of knowing and using the System is justified.

Along with the Pavlovian social engineers like Pointsman, Pynchon suggests that the Slothrop line has lost its concern for the Preterite and become a part of the They System, the self-annointed Controllers of individual human destinies. Tyrone Slothrop's immediate forebears were connected with the development of monopoly capitalism in the first part of the twentieth century, demonstrating the Max Weber hypothesis that Calvinism shifted in its emphasis from purity of spirit to pride in industry and wealth as evidence of spiritual election.

Tyrone's sense of guilt at what his ancestors have wrought and his need to find his own place in the shaky scheme of things leads him to the discovery (invention) of his own family's connections with the international conglomerate that helped to develop the Hitler war machine, IG Farben. He believes that as an infant he was given to its chief scientist, Lazlo Jamf, and was conditioned by him.

Slothrop is supposedly assigned by Allied intelligence to the task of locating the guidance device for the German rockets, the *S-Gerät* (or *Schwartzgerät*, the black, or primitive and instinctive, directing apparatus), the existence of which is highly problematic since the early German rockets needed no such device to accomplish their random bombing of England. Slothrop's quest for the *S-Gerät* is like Stencil's quest for V. and Oedipa's quest for the Trystero, a quest for meaning that projects its own possible answer. It is also a search using the intellectual means of study and detection that intelligence demands. Slothrop in this quest is at the service of Them.

A point of awakening for Slothrop occurs when, hard on the trail of the mysterious German rocket device, he reads in the London *Times* that his closest friend, Tantivy, has been killed in the war. Tantivy has apparently been sent to his death by the same people who control Slothrop's activities as an Allied intelligence agent. Slothrop has also just discovered that Imipolex-G, an important plastic in the construction of the rocket, was manufactured by Shell, and that the Shell Oil Building across the channel has a German rocket on top of it while the British retain a heavy financial interest in Shell Oil. The war, in this novel, as in Joseph Heller's absurd novel *Catch-22*, is essentially a war for markets and capital.

As early as *V.*, Pynchon makes the connection between capitalism, technology, and warfare. In that novel Bloody Chiclitz presides over Yoyodyne, an aerospace manufacturing conglomerate that started out as a toy company. Its engineer, who came from Sothwest Africa and worked in Germany on V-1 and V-2 rockets, is Kurt Mondaugen, whose studies of "noise" from out space *(sferics)* enabled his superior, Weissman, to finagle out Ludwig Wittgenstein's skeptical dictum: "The world is all that the case is."[13] *Weissman* ("white man") is introduced again in *Gravity's Rainbow* where his character is delineated through the reading of tarot cards. The overall delineation is that of the decadent white Anglo-Saxon Protestant, unsure of himself sexually, addicted to material comforts, ulcerous, revering youth, wanting knowledge, and fearful of death.[14]

With a loss of faith in a superior spiritual intelligence, the world is viewed as a closed system. We know only what our senses permit us to perceive and what the operations of logic permit us to connect together. Life then becomes a game to be played for its own sake and a system or set of systems to be discovered, invented, and manipulated, in Nietzschean terms, by the human will beyond good and evil. There is no accountability outside the system, and no purpose beyond itself. Life in the view of the more passive, someone like Jessica Swanlake, becomes not a great historic struggle between good and evil but is merely to be lived "until something falls."[15]

For the activist, the situation calls for the construction of one's own self-sufficient system within the larger societal one or the instigation of a countering social system that may replace or reform the larger one. Pirate Prentice, Slothrop's fellow intelligence officer, tells Slothrop that those who are able to identify with their fellows and who have compassion need to form a We System to counter the They System of impersonal human exploitation. As in *The Crying of Lot 49,* the counterforce is one of spontaneous human feeling.

The They System can be wrecked by refusing to accept its premise that thought must be rational and in accord with accepted principles of order. If irrationality has to be accepted as a truth, a necessary part of reality, then the They System, unable to incorporate such an idea logically, will paralyze and disintegrate. Osbie Feel, the film director, wears a Porky Pig tattoo on his stomach (a sign of his rebellion on behalf of the Preterite) and proclaims the We System as gloriously irrational and opposed to the interlocking thought patterns of the They System.

What makes it difficult to free oneself from the control of the They System is that

> the Man has a branch office in each of our brains, his corporate emblem is a white albatross, each local rep has a cover known as the Ego, and their mission in this world is Bad Shit. We do know what's going on, and we let it go on. As long as we can see them, stare at them, those massively moneyed, once in a while. As long as they allow us a glimpse, however rarely. We need that.[16]

Pynchon says that we are subtly programmed by the They System and that we only know it when the programming lapses. We, in such moments of "neglect," are suddenly in tune with our own deepest, normally repressed needs and feelings.[17]

Slothrop, looking back to his Harvard past, wonders if Malcolm (Malcolm X) the shoe shine boy, Slothrop, and Jack Kennedy, senior at Harvard, were ever lined up in the men's toilet there, "sitting, squatting, and passing through." Kennedy and Malcolm were both murdered, and "They" are ever after Slothrop. Slothrop's quest for freedom is thus attached to a larger societal quest, and the source of Slothrop's "paranoia" is given very large political dimensions.[18]

The They System is dedicated to the mechanization of society. It would produce an endless replication of Clive Mossmoons, individuals who serve without joy, only fulfilling the demands of the operation, expendable pieces in a game that continues.[19] Such a System is the result of man's increasing reliance on technology to create a comfortable, orderly universe. The thinking that promotes such a system is shown in the lectures of Professor Lazlo Jamf, inventor of Imipolex G. Jamf told his students at the Technology Institute to develop the compounds of Silicon, Boron, and Phosphorus in bonds with Nitrogen, replacing Hydrogen, replacing life with the inorganic. "Here is no frailty, no mortality—here is Strength and the Timeless," Jamf said and then wiped the C-H off the blackboard, to replace those "Christian" letters with the symbols for Silicon and Nitrogen, Si—N.[20]

At a seance the medium contacts the spirit of Walter Rathenau, a Jew, technologist, and assassinated foreign minister of the Weimar Republic. He tells the assembled German corporate technologists that technology has made man think that he can synthesize and control things in all situations and that in so doing he is creating a new life, but all this scientific activity merely leads to death transformed, a world of things given new physical properties. His audience reacts with cynical laughter.[21]

Human life is or should be a break with, and felt separation from, the inanimate, the unconscious, and the mechanistic. As the life force becomes more and more channeled into rote patterns of response, consciousness, which depends upon movement, opposition, and change, becomes threatened, the sense of self narrows, and the personality becomes mechanized and rigid like Pointsman's or Jeremy's. For those who find the patterns of response required of them in conflict with their needs for personal love and individual purpose, the personal response is one either of flight or rebellion. When pressed too closely and with the avenues of escape all but closed, the personality disintegrates. Flight, rebellion, disintegration, and a return to wholeness are the stages of Slothrop's opposition to the inanimate and of his quest for transcendence.

One of the first views we get of Slothrop under stress is as he is hugging a child during a rocket attack, and is finally blessed with her Shirley Temple smile.[22] His role as a preserver of innocence, love, and possiblity in an absurd, warring world is established. He reminds one of J.D. Salinger's soldier in "For Esmé—with Love and Squalor," where the little girl Esmé gives him hope to go on at a time when his sense of purpose is flagging.

It is 1944 and Slothrop has not cleaned out his desk since 1942. He is fatigued and feels trapped in an inhuman state of affairs. He tries, initially, to escape from his fear and from a sense of isolation through numerous sexual affairs. After it is discovered that his chart of conquests resembles the pattern of V-2 strikes and Pointsman has put him under the influence of sodium amytol to discover what he knows about the coincidence, his escape takes the form of hallucinations, in which he is feeling the presence of black men in a lavatory and pursuing his dropped harmonica, called a mouth harp, down a toilet. The harp, of course, has spiritual connotations. It is also a means of self-expression as a musical instrument, and in size and shape it is close to being a phallus. It is his lost spiritual, creative, and effective self that he is chasing from that moment forward until the recovery of that "harp" after his last escape from Pointsman's clutches and the substitution of Major Marvy's castration for his own.

Early in his assigned search for evidence of the S-Gerät Slothrop visits the sites of rocket explosions and thinks of himself as St. George poking around for droppings of the Beast that is no more. The Devil is not as easily identified, let alone vanquished, in Slothrop's hallucinatory century as he was in the visions of Slothrop's Puritan ancestors. Throughout his adventures Slothrop is a kind of knight-errant on a quest that may prove futile. Much later in the novel Slothrop is wearing a pig suit like a knight's armor and carrying a plastic knight (a chess piece), which gains him entrance to Putzi's palace of vice and revelry on a stretch of beach reaching out into the North Sea toward Helgoland (toward damnation). There he is succored by the maiden Solange, and his enemy Major Marvy is carted off to be castrated in his stead. Knighthood has become not a matter of manly virtues but a kind of plucky faith, to be rewarded eventually by the rough balancing-out of chance encounters.

Putzi's is almost too much for Slothrop. He retreats to a closet and sucks the ear of his costume pig head. But Solange (the angelic masseuse) and Pig Bodine (one of *V.'s* major Preterite characters) bring him out of it. Bodine says that everything is a plot of some kind, and Solange illustrates with her "red-pointed finger vectors" that extend in all directions. Slothrop realizes for the first time "that the Zone can sustain many other plots besides those polarizing upon himself." At this point the personal guilt Slothrop feels for what his ancestry has become, the moral decline from spirituality to materialism, eases as he sees his Puritan self in the larger context of human history. He now sees the Zone as an enormous transit system and that, by riding appropriate distances and by knowing when to transfer, he may yet find freedom. He decides to travel with Pig Bodine and Solange now for a while (a transfer).[23]

When Mark Twain wrote "What Is Man?" in the later years after his bankruptcy and family illnesses, he concluded that man was a happiness and suffering machine, and that, over all, the two emotions balanced out but that hope kept him going. So it is in the absurdity of a world where allies are allied to the enemy and the enemy is as human or inhuman as ourselves. And in the fatalistic Zone Slothrop concludes that there is a rough kind of balance between justice and injustice. Pointsman's conditioning of Slothrop fails and so does his plot to sterilize him. Instead, Pointsman's *gung ho* Major Marvy is castrated under the "radiant eye" of the ambulance dome light as though some witnessing God were redressing the balance for poor pigheaded Slothrop.

While Marvy is being castrated, Slothrop is lying beside Solange (who is really Leni, another of Pynchon's guises of eternal woman), and she is dreaming of her child Ilse on a freight train escaping Them: "She will not be used. There is change and departure: but there is also help when least looked for from strangers of the day, and hiding out among the accidents of this drifting Humility, never quite to be extinguished, a few small chances for mercy. . . ."[24]

The Zone is not designed to preserve one's innocence, but even the young can survive, somehow. Ludwig and his lemming do so. "Ludwig has fallen into a state worse than death and found it's negotiable. So not all lemmings go over the cliff, and not all children are preserved against snuggling into the sin of profit. To expect any more, or less, of the Zone is to disagree with the terms of the Creation."[25] Pynchon acknowledges man's ability to survive even the most corrupt situations. If morality is no refuge, then man's vitality, ingenuity, and willingness to negotiate to mutual advantage is. Ludwig has prostituted himself, but he has survived, and what else, under the circumstances, could one ask him to do?

The world is Darwinian, governed by a competition for survival, but individuals can learn to join forces to compete more effectively. Ludwig learns that early. Slothrop at various times finds himself traveling with black marketeers and with a cocaine peddler. He sleeps with a woman who has been partly responsible for the internment of Jews. The Preterite have much in common, no matter what their particular vices, and they are able to persevere only through these temporary alliances, and knowing when to "transfer."

Mere survival is not enough, however. Man longs to transcend this imperfect state of existence, to become the one in control instead of the one controlled, to "strike through the pasteboard mask" that the supreme intelligence wears, as Herman Melville said in *Moby Dick*,[26] or to become all knowing, one with the very life of things," a "transparent eyeball" in Emerson's terms. In *V.* Pynchon examined the various manifestations of the *élan vital* and, like Bergson, he concluded that the scientific mode of thinking is dangerously mechanistic and that to appreciate life in its fullness one must rely upon intuition and its sense of things as a whole lasting through time.

In *V.* there is a repetition and endurance of V. through generations. Sidney Stencil feels a great nostalgia about the scene on Malta; it is Florence all over again with V. present now in an older guise, talk of revolution, and a mixture of priests, politics, and sex. Malta is the rock, enduring, all-life-encompassing. Its sage is Fausto Maijstral, son of an earlier Fausto, and the only survivor of the generation of 1937. He is one who would have been a priest, whose brothers are a politician and an engineer. Fausto IV, as he calls himself, is now a man of letters and covers all the areas of knowledge. (The parallels to the Pynchon lineage probably suggest somewhat the author's intent in the introduction of Fausto and his statements about Malta.) Fausto poetizes the inanimate and tries to make the world amenable to men's wishes. Pynchon views the poet as a kind of noble liar, as did Plato, long before. Maijstral's Malta is a kind of Rock of Ages, the faith alive in its deep clefts, a long-violated woman impervious to the assaults upon her, full of faith and part of the earth. Fausto's vision is intuitive, healing, and holistic.

In Pynchon's early story, "Entropy," there are a group of musicians who play mental music, without instruments, keying into one another's feelings and intuitively pantomiming their playing. In *The Crying of Lot 49* Oedipa's disc jockey husband Mucho Maas, ashamed of his car-selling past and not believing in the flipped-out jargon of his rock music, has come to believe that if people could "hear" one another as instruments playing together that this would be a sort of communion that would establish love in the world. His wife Oedipa goes on a quest for signs which takes her through a surrealistic set of experiences in the streets, cafés, and flophouses of San Narciso. She comforts a sick drunk only to have him call her a bitch. But then she ends in a dance with deaf mutes, who dance each according to the music in his head, all without colliding, like the dance of the spheres. The suggestion throughout is that all the apparent conflict and opposition appears to be our reality because the Whole is only partly understood, that an understanding of the Whole can only be intuitive. Formal communication and its attendant intellectual processes foster the sense of conflict.

The analytic and intuitive modes of thought are opposed throughout Pynchon's work, often in the same character. Oedipa's search for the Trystero is inspired by an intuitive sense that there is a principle of freedom and spontaneity in life that has to be in revolt against the increasingly rigid systems of its social institutions. Her method of discovery, however, according to Driblett, is too analytical, her demand for signs too exact. In *Gravity's Rainbow* Weissman, the analytic administrator, becomes Blicero, seeker after Godhead, sacrificing his "son" Gottfried (the name is, of course, symbolic) to his dream of man's union with the spiritual. Slothrop too goes from analytic student of rocketry to quester after spirituality. Early in the novel he becomes so lost in the intellectual quest for understanding the workings of the rocket's machinery that he alienates Katje, his love, and the fullest emanation of eternal woman in all of Pynchon. Later, he comes to see the rocket in spiritual terms and is brought back to wholeness with the love of woman and a kind of Taoist, intuitive acceptance of the cosmos.

Slothrop's search for the *Schwartzgerät* of the V-2 (the technological emanation of a now all but completely mechanized and inanimate V, or life force) is like Stencil's search for V., and Oedipa's search for the Trystero, a search for an operative spiritual force. The Puritans believed that the world was God's creation and that the mind of the Creator and His divine order could be revealed through the word of God as revealed to His prophets and through the discovery of analogues in the workings of nature (hence the interest in science on the part of divines such as Cotton Mather and Jonathan Edwards). Some like Anne Hutchinson also believed in divine revelation to the laity. In the nineteenth century the Unitarian-then-Transcendentalist Emerson preached the existence of an Oversoul to be discovered in nature, but it was also Emerson in his later years who came to question whether man could ever comprehend the divine order in history's infinite series, with no definite beginning or end. By the middle of the nineteenth century the idea of a moral universe was no longer an article of faith among many intellectuals. It was a matter of investigation and speculation. Melville, Twain, and Henry Adams illustrate the shift over the succeeding years past the turn of the century. Pynchon continues the quest into the second half of the twentieth century.

Stencil, whose very name may be construed as "a metaphor for the attempt to find meaning in history, can ultimately reveal only the shape of desire, the pattern in the artifice," Charles Russell notes in a cogent critique of Pynchon's language.[27] At the end of Herbert Stencils' father's life Sidney Stencil is waiting on Malta with Veronica, an emanation of V. as caring love, living a secluded, orderly life, awaiting the outcome of the June assembly, hopeful of an independent Malta. But Malta finally votes three to one to be part of the British Empire. As of 1956 Malta was still not self-ruling, any more than man is really self-dependent, though he too endures. On the tenth of June 1919, as the Paris Peace Conference drew to a close and President Woodrow Wilson returned to the United States, Sidney Stencil, foreign service officer of America's age of innocence, is swept up by a waterspout out of a cloudless sky off the Maltese coast. Did Stencil transcend the operations of V. or did he merely die?

The question is suggested again, less hopefully, in Gottfried's last moments aboard the rocket in *Gravity's Rainbow*. Gottfried tries to hold onto images of life, but all turns white as he reaches the apex of the rocket's trajectory and the supposed point of illumination, which simply wipes out everything except the image of people's hopes left him by Blicero. As the rocket with Gottfried in it comes rushing down over the movie house of life's hopeful projections at the close of the novel, we are asked to join in a hymn of old William Slothrop's, and lest we think it more than an exercise of togetherness, we are asked to "follow the bouncing ball" as moviegoers did in days of yore, as the imaged ball pointed to the words on the screen that were to be sung in mindless good spirit.

The interpretations of history given by Max Weber and Henry Adams, which are central to *V.*'s narrative and to its metaphoric development, are still effective in *Gravity's Rainbow*, but to them surely should be added the works of T.S. Eliot, Sigmund Freud, and Carl Jung. This is not to say that these are the only significant influences. Pynchon is throughly imbued with the intellectual thought of or time. These works, however, do provide us with many of the basic threads to Pynchon's own tower tapestry, his own *Weltanschauung*, especially where religions and the the human psyche are concerned.

Like Freud, Pynchon finds God an illusion, an outgrowth of the libido's quest for life-extension. To make his point he used Eliot's *Waste Land* images to his own ends; for instance, the whiteness of the moment of ecstatic revelation in Eliot becomes merely an obliteration of all except the images of hope. (Compare Eliot's Hyacinth girl passage in *The Waste Land* with Gottfried's rocket solo.)

Pynchon has also borrowed Eliot's tarot cards, and with them he gives us the effete character of the WASP in laying out Weissman's (Blicero's) cards and the terrible sense of impotence that lies at the heart of Slothrop's personality disintegration from the time he creates his slapstick superman role as Rocketman to his healing dream of the rainbow cock. His tarot card self has cards that are reversed, pointing only to "a long and scuffling future." Slothrop at this point in his adventures in the Zone calls himself Ian Scuffling and passes himself off as a newspaper "correspondent." He is however, still Puritan William Slothrop's descendent, seeking "correspondences" between the intelligence that produced the rocket and that of the Master of the universe. His Hanged Man card is reversed too, right side up. The Hanged Man upside down is a symbol of rebirth, the god's sacrifice for renewed fertility. Slothrop's future holds no rebirth. He is reduced to the "telling of his secret hopes and fears," like Eliot's Prufrock.[28]

This is not to say that Pynchon finds no validity in religion.It is not only a natural emanation of man's desire for transcendence, an extension of the life force, but it also sets for us ideals of conduct that we ignore at our peril. What makes the Zone so dangerous is that without law, both civil and religious having been based on religious tradition, everyone must fend for himself, and the world becomes a flux of amoral,*ad hoc* alliances and selfish opportunism.

The spokesman for the Counterforce says that communion is communion with one's enemy. To drink of the Grail is to drink the blood of one's enemy.[29] The connection of the religious ceremony to a pagan war rite is recognition that there is that within us that is opposed to the Christian way of life, but that the opposition also inspires hope for union.

Man's selfishness and his competitive instinct blind him to the opportunities for human love. So it is that Enzian, the Christian Herrero, meets his Marxist half brother Tchitcherine and, while giving him a pack of cigarettes, still fails to recognize him. Enzian also takes long walks with the boy Christian. Both see that they cannot protect people from the rocket (and from man's destructive reaching for personal power over the cosmos that it stands for). Enzian feels that he must, however, pass on his knowledge to Christian so that, hopefully, out of the knowledge of man's suffering, faith in Christian love (the Counterforce) may be reborn.

Unfortunately, even if God were to give a sign, it would probably be ignored, as Slothrop ignores the crosses of windmills in a smoke-covered sky, though they might be "spoke-blurs of the terrible Rider himself."[30] Some who do seek the sign are absurd, like the undertaker in his metal suit in a boat at sea during a thunderstorm, seeking to be struck by lightning so that he may have "special knowledge" that will help him in his business.

Equally absurd are those who seek sanctity through heroic right action. Slothrop falls overboard trying to save the supposedly innocent Bianca, thrown off a white ship, the *Anubis,* into a white sea, a white nothingness as opposed to Eliot's white illumination once again. He is rescued by the terrible mistress of a ship trading in the black market, Frau Gnahb. His first feeling about Katje, the world-wise double agent, is that she is an innocent, but after lying with her, his clothes are stolen and he chases the thief up a tree only to fall into the middle of a croquet game, draped in a purple cloth, innocent young Slothrup losing his innocence. He should have known better, for when Katje first presented herself to him naked, she showed a whiter than white back but a dark front and a face that became a muzzle. Katje throughout is a kind of nymph-goddess, a continuation of the ambivalent woman motif that runs through the character of V., alternate aspects of the life force and eternal woman.[31]

Sexual love, though a primal expression of the libido, is not the way to oneness with the Infinite either. Slothrop's sexual arousal is thought to be a result of Professor Jamf's early conditioning when he was a child. Supposedly, Slothrop has erections in response to the proximity of Imipolex-G, a plastic used in the V-2. When coupling with Geli Tripping, it is Wernher the owl jumping on his back that makes him ejaculate (Wernher Von Braun firing another rocket). Slothrop comes to think of himself as programmed by Them and to see even his sex life in those terms. Among the other characters, the V-2 engineering genius Pökler's sex life is controlled by Them, and his erections require pornographic movies.

Slothrop, in any case, is an inconstant lover. Pynchon critic George Levine puts it this way:

> Unanchored to a past which has been invented and programmed for him, increasingly losing his connection with a future that was only a rocket, Slothrop finds no way to make love a part of his life beyond that instant when it happens. He cannot hold both the moment and the memory. Slothrop's orgasm with Bianca comes in the shape of a rocket, like a rocket it explodes, destroys, ends.[32]

For the moment his love is all-consuming. He is all cock, "inside his cock," for love of Bianca, but he will leave after loving her, and because of his inconstancy in his love of the child-innocent, unlike Tannhauser, the Pope's staff will not flower for him.[33] Love, as most humans know it, is attachment and dependence, and as such it is antithetical to the ideal of unfettered, free, self-realization and transcendence over worldly attachments.[34]

As early as his story "Low-Lands," Pynchon envisioned the man-woman relationship as both mutually protective and mutually exclusive. His hero, Dennis Flange, flees his wife Cindy to seek the comfort of old shipmates in a garbage dump, a place to dump his cares. There he spirals to the dead center of the dump and thinks of the dump changing, flattening out to a kind of lowland plain. (Lowlands, crossroads, and interfaces are all transition points in Pynchon.) The plain finally shrinks to convexity, leaving him sticking out, unsheltered. The fear of man's alienation from the protective concern of his wife during her pregnancy is symbolized. His reconciliation to the idea of her having a child is shown in his dream as he lies between his two old shipmates. It is a dream in which he retreats under the dump with a childwoman and her childlike rat. She is identified with the all-accepting fertile and mysterious sea, for her eyes are full of white caps, and sea creatures are "cruising about in the submarine green of her heart."

In that same germinal story Flange finds that the ocean has a kind of solidity. "For Flange that immense cloud-glass plain was a kind of lowland which almost demanded a single human figure striding across it for completeness." The single human figure would be male, of course, for the male principle of life is that of separateness and a thrusting out beyond the known. The woman, on the other hand, is not simply self-contained. She needs man for completeness, as the ocean needs the land.[35]

Slothrop's first view of Katje is as Venus coming out of the sea. She is playing a role, however, and is not a goddess of love. She has "the soft nose of a doe, eyes behind blonde lashes full of acid green," and a "thin-lipped European mouth."[36] Slothrop soon learns that his Venus is in the service of Pointsman. She is, nonetheless, V. Like the Colonial Victoria Wren of *V.* she is the woman who both succors and devours. She is closer to her biological, earthly purpose than the intellectual Slothrop, and when he becomes immersed in the study of rocketry (technology's sexual sublimation) and fails to attend to her needs, Katje leaves him. Several pages later, after Webley Silvernail's celebration of animal grace and lament over Technology's dictatorship over the mind of man, as he communes with his animals in the laboratory of the psychological warfare organization known as the White Visitation, Katje wreaks her revenge on the separating force of man's search for transcendence. In what has to be the most intentionally disgusting scene in all of Pynchon, she dominates the head of the White Visitation, old Brigadier Pudding, making him, out of his lust and need for punishment drink her urine and eat her feces.

Edwin Fussell says that Pudding's act is symbolic of his consistent mental return to the Great War and his inability to ever see it clearly.[37] Pointsman too is an anal-erotic character, happy only when standing in the corner (as he would have when punished as a boy) or symbolically stomping around in the ruins of a V-2 strike with a ruined commode stuck on his foot, looking for dogs to perform his conditioning experiments on. No less Slothrop, sliding down the toilet after his mouth harp.

Western man's prideful sense of self and quest for individual heroism and self-extension Pynchon seems to trace back to Puritan idealism and repression. They make Western man unable to come to terms with the need to be a part, sexually, socially, and psychologically, of what is essentially a biological enterprise, social life. Katje clearly sees Slothrop's rocket-mania as a substitute for sex, for herself. For Katje, the rocket burning at takeoff is like a peacock fanning its tail (a show of male pride) and suggestive in its multiplicity of colors of Godolphin's ethereal vision of Vheissu in *V.*. The rocket's arc she sees as "a clear allusion to certain secret lusts that drive the planet herself, and Those who use her—over its peak and down, plunging, burning, toward terminal orgasm. . . ."[38]

Much earlier, in the story "Entropy" (1960), Pynchon was telling us that life and love cannot successfully be nurtured in an intellectual hothouse. Life managed, controlled, and structured, as the intellectual Callisto tries to make it in his temperature-controlled apartment, eventually stifles the spirit, symbolized by the bird in the story. Downstairs, just off the street, Meatball Mulligan permits his party guests to make a shambles of his apartment but then sets to straightening it up afterward.[39] We need to keep order as best we can, without artificiality, with adequate outlet for both the drives of Eros (love, union, order, and creativity) and of Thanatos (hate, aggression, dissolution, and destruction).

In *Gravity's Rainbow* it is the force of gravity that assures the maintenance of a balance between the forces of Eros and Thanatos, forces inherent in the rocket's creation and purpose. In that book Nora Dodson-Truck sees herself as the force of gravity: "That against which the Rocket must struggle, to which the prehistoric wastes submit and are transmuted to the very substance of History. . . ."[40] Other women characters also oppose the rocket. Katje and Leni Pökler cannot accept the rocket as transcendence, though Leni's father-lover Pökler and Weissman do. She calls such thinking *Kadavergehorsamkeit* ("collective death").[41] She sees very clearly that this *Schwarmerei* ("enthusiasm for an ideal") is really Thanatos, that it threatens to destroy the very forces of life that created it. Woman, corrupt though she may be in Pynchon, continues to be the protector of life.

Stencil in *V.,* discouraged in his pursuit of meaning, asks wise Fausto if he is after his own extermination, and Fausto replies by gesturing toward Valletta. "Ask her," he whispered. "Ask the Rock."[42] The death wish is not unnatural. It is as natural as volcanic eruptions and other destructive forces in the universe, which though destructive of life are only transformational in terms of physical nature.

Lyle Bland, successful industrialist, and the one who was instrumental in giving the infant Slothrop to Jamf for conditioning, becomes a Mason, and under the tutelage of mystics and sensitives he finally wills himself to death. Late in life Bland is rejecting the wastefulness of industry and unconsciously affirming the vision of Kekulé, discoverer of the benzene ring and father of organic chemistry. In the vision, as Pynchon interprets it, a serpent announces, "The World is a closed thing, cyclical, resonant, eternally returning."[43] Bland appears to understand man's efforts at transcendence through technology are wrong-headed, that life cannot be successfully extended and lastingly improved at the expense of its inanimate, natural counterpart.

The inanimate gives the rise to the animate and reclaims it once again. The inanimate is not forever fixed, however. It is a constant combining and recombining of molecules. It has its own energies, out of which the animate sprang (or so it appears within the limits of perception that bound the closed system of human consciousness and its speculations concerning history and evolution).

Bland thinks of himself as journeying out of his body on longer and longer trips and finally leaving forever. Blicero is no less mystical, but more religious, regarding the soul's flight. In readying his lover and sacrificial son, Gottfried, for his flight aboard the rocket, Blicero speaks a rambling monologue on America. America, he says, is the Edge and Death Europe sought. The moon is the new

Edge and Death. He also speaks of his vision of filmlike people shot long ago from Earth, now living in a closed sphere in space. This picture of a strange human decadence is the end of the human aspiration for transcendence. Then he says to Gottfried: "I want to break out—to leave this cycle of infection and death. I want to be taken in love: so taken that you and I, and death, and life, will be gathered, inseparable, into the radiance of what we could become..."[44] Blicero is reminiscent of the Puritan divines kneeling on hard floors beseeching God to enter their hearts and consume their lives, uniting them with Godhead. Like Abraham he will sacrifice his Isaac to prove his devotion and through him be blessed.

This scene, Pynchon tells us, "must be read as a card: what is to come." It is a scene assignable anywhere in the deck, "like the Fool." It is a scene of man's hope of spiritual transcendence, the placement of which with other cards gives him a chance of holding a winning hand, but it turns up irregularly, and the winning is never constant. Man is a fool of his hopes, indeed Fortune's fool.

One might say that Blicero chooses a strange way to find his Nirvana, but he is, after all, Technology's child, so much that Nirvana is envisioned as a media message, two-dimensional and empty. It is Thanatz much earlier who has explained the rocket's own place in the mystic quest. Speaking of the A-4 rocket, he tells Slothrop, "...it really did possess a Max Weber charisma...some joyful—and deeply irrational—force the state bureaucracy could never routinize, against which it could not prevail. . . . they did resist it, but they also allowed it to happen. We cannot imagine anyone *choosing* a role like that. But every year, somehow, their numbers grow."[45] The bureaucracy is dominated by men like Blicero, highly repressed, half in love with death, perhaps in the final stage of the white man's (Weissman's) evolution.

Blicero indulges in sodomy with Gottfried while Katje looks on. He looks at life as a Hansel and Gretel myth, fearing his own death in the oven as the "children"revolt. Blicero's hatred of woman and his attempt to recreate his own youth in homosexual acts are signs of his overwhelming desire to be a god unto himself. Gottfried is shot to the heavens shrouded in Imipolex, Jamf's sexually arousing plastic, as a kind of love offering to a vengeful Jehovah. Only Blicero's lover in the *Sudwest,* a Herrero boy he called Enzian after the Gentian in Rilke's *Duino Elegies,* fucked without guilt, for the Herrero god, unlike the white man's was one that held all opposites as part of his being—creation, destruction, and sex were One. It is no accident then that the repressed Weissman becomes the most selfish and destructive Blicero while the pagan Herrero becomes the most Christ-like Enzian.

The male quest for transcendence in Western society is very much in the service of Thanatos, the death wish, because of the Puritan denial of human instinct. Thanatz whips Greta Erdmann and, in so doing, makes himself feel free of earthly bonds, ready for escape. He finds such joy in his actions that he feels it unfair that sadomasochism should be the prerogative of the elite. As far as

Thanatz is concerned, we are all sadomasochistic and should be allowed guilt-free self-indulgence. He does not seem to take into account that such extreme forms of sadism as he indulges in or as Blicero indulges in *require* a deep sense of guilt for the pleasure they give.[46]

Sadomasochistic expressions of puritan guilt abound in Pynchon. The children's dismantling of the Bad Priest in *V.* is a foreshadowing of more lively scenes in *Gravity's Rainbow*. When Greta Erdmann spanks Bianca for refusing to act out a part on the ship *Anubis,* all the bystanders are aroused to sadistic, masochistic, anal, and oral intercourse except a Japanese liaison man, who merely looks on with the acceptance of a Herrero god, or an Oriental Siva. In the Zone, Slothrop is constantly aroused, and those around him are constantly buggering and inflicting sexual cruelties, a perverted expression of frustrated potency all the way around. When the Japanese, Ensign Morituri, is later asked why he does not join in, he says he would feel *"more alone"* if he did.[47] These are violent acts of frustration in a guilt-ridden, predatory society. Morituri, who wants only to return to his family in lovely Hiroshima, would alienate himself from his culture were he to "join in." The activities at Putzi's, Brigadier Pudding's "feast," and the buggering of Gottfried first by Thanatz and then by Blicero, Pökler's incest with Leni, and the whipping of Katje and Greta stand out as other examples of violent, guilt-twisted ("kinky") sex.

Pynchon does not condemn homosexuality *per se.* But homosexuality, which might have been merely an extension of a respectful homoeroticism during and before World War I, has become "bitchery" in World War II.[48] Certainly, as we see it in *Gravity's Rainbow,* homosexuality is a kind of objectified narcissism, an all-consuming love of self, that is sterile, leading to fetishism and death. So it has been before in *V.* with the love of V. and Melanie L'Heuremaudit: "Dead at last, they would be one with the inanimate universe and with each other. Love-play until then thus becomes an impersonation of the inanimate, a transvestism not between sexes but between quick and dead; human and fetish."[49] So it is too in Blicero's relationship to Gottfried, who becomes Blicero's ideal, plastic-wrapped, ejaculation into nothingness.

The violence in sexual relationships becomes further ritualized in instances of mass violence. In Pynchon's early story, "Mortality and Mercy in Vienna," Irving Loon's mass killing of the decadents in the Rumanian's apartment is done under the eye of a pig fetus as a ritual act of cleansing, what Pynchon calls a "eucharistic miracle."[50] In *V.* Stencil Senior tells us, regarding a possible revolution on Malta in 1919, that "mob violence, like tourism is a kind of communion. By its special magic large numbers of lonely souls, however heterogeneous, can share the common property of opposition to what is."[51] In *Gravity's Rainbow* Foppl's mass killings of blacks in Southwest Africa gave him a sense of communion based on a feeling of joint disregard for human life, theirs, his, all men's—a merging with the inanimate.[52]

The murderers excuse their act as necessary for the realization of the ideal. The old foreign officer Stencil once wrote in his journal:

> If there is any political moral to be found in this world, it is that we carry on the business of this century with an intolerable double vision. Right and Left; the Hothouse and the Street. The Right can only live and work hermetically in the hothouse of the past, while outside the Left prosecute their affairs in the streets by manipulated mob violence. And cannot live but in the dreamscape of the future.[53]

It is the "dreamscape of the future" that lures us on to desperate acts and makes us impatient enough with the present to destroy it. Western man is a captive of time and of the notion of inevitable progress to eventual perfection.

In some degree Pynchon views progress dialectically, as a growing opposition of forces that reach a stage where there is synthesis. The synthesis then becomes a new premise that creates its own opposition, and so on. It is a Hegelian process. The conflict between religion and science leads to a kind of mysticized technology. The conflict between man as transformer of life and woman as protector of it leads to repression, guilt, homosexuality, and sadomasochism; the conflict of the intellect and the instincts likewise, the conflict between a quest for pure spirit and the demands of bodily satisfactions likewise. We appear to be trebly damned in our very natures, though, of course, the last two conflicts are really factors of the first sexual equation. The general lack of *caritas* and the triumph of self-love in the present give rise to the "counterforce," Oedipa's Trystero (an anarchistic, Edenic love) or Enzian's all-accepting Herrero (Christian) kind of love. The synthesis of these opposites is yet to come. The mysticized technology expresses the most potentially dangerous form of self-love as Weissman-Blicero amply demonstrates. The feeble religious response to the threat at the end of *Gravity's Rainbow* is a parody of a dialectical opposite that has run its course. If the "counterforce" is too weak, then the final synthesis will be annihilation and union with the inanimate.

Religion in our time has been replaced with faith in Technology. Slothrop's spiritual father is Professor Jamf. At one point he camps next to Jamf's crypt, hoping for a spiritual communication, but unlike Christ, Jamf is only dead. Slothrop's analyst later tells him that he is fascinated by the rocket because he is secretly in love with his race's death. Slothrop is imbued with a destructive guilt for his ancestors' materialism, capitalistic corruption, and greed, and, in fact, for the sins of the white race as a whole. The flight of the rocket promises escape and its crashing return fitting annihilation.

As Gottfried rises in the rocket, we are told: "This ascent will be betrayed to Gravity. But the Rocket engine, the deep cry of combustion that jars the soul, promises escape. The victim in bondage to falling, rises on a promise, a prophecy of Escape. . . ."[54] The desire is for full awareness, full consciousness, eternal and harmonious. Tyrone Slothrop has thought of it as a "keying into waves," which he thinks of as a way of leaving forever, as Lyle Bland thought of doing on his "journeys."[55]

Slothrop does not leave forever, we know. He is one of the Preterite, forced to suffer the indignities of a technologized world in which the individual is, as Mexico points out, merely a part of the statistical order of things. Slothrop loses what sense of belonging he has when he realizes that he is being manipulated by Them within a system that allows him little real personal freedom. His anomie is described in electronic media terms, as though he is not really human but only an image of humanity, a transformation of technology, like the automatons SHROUD and SHOCK in the earlier novel *V.*

Arriving at Peenemunde, passing the rocket sites (the stations of the cross) Slothrop approaches the Holy Center, and as he does so, he has already begun to "scatter," decreasing his "temporal bandwidth," his "personal density." He is more and more in a narrower Now with little sense of cause or possibility, past or future. There is a loss of self, a disintegration, as he reaches the place of the Rocket's genesis. In his disintegration Bodine offers the failed Rocketman a cloth soaked in the blood of John Dillinger (Christ's robe, with Christ as rebel, freedom's martyr). Bodine says he does not need it, for he is out of the Dumbo stage, suggesting that the failed knight, Slothrop is still in it. What they all need, Bodine says, is "grace. The physical grace to keep it working." "It" is the force of *caritas,* and Pig Bodine is its earthy spokesman.[56]

In his travels in the Zone, instead of a Kilroy symbol Slothrop leaves a rocket symbol. It is a technologized cross and sign of the Holy Center. The Kilroy symbol Pynchon says was inspired by a band pass filter. The human face with a nose "flirting with castration" was only a metaphor. Both symbols represent the desire for escape, the "decreasing of temporal bandwidth," and suggest a frustrated potency.

Slothrop finds bagpipes left behind by a Highland unit and begins playing them. Once again in tune with the comradery of a soldierly Preterite, he is ready for his own self-assertion. He picks his old mouth harp out of a mountain stream and thinks of Rilke's lines:

> And though earthliness forget you,
> To the stilled earth say: I flow.
> To the rushing water speak: I am.[57]

Later he dreams of being hung like the hanged god of Sir James Frazer's *Golden Bough.* As he is hung, he has an erection, and his sperm drops to the ground to seed a mandrake. A magician pulls it out and the magician's black dog also dies sacrificially. The miraculous mandrake (the creation of sacrifice) is sought for by the capitalists to make money. After the recognition that there must be death to produce life, that creation entails pain and death, and that our civilization seeks a cheap happiness without the sacrifice, Slothrop feels a cleansing rain and has a vision of a "stout rainbow cock... driven into the wet-valleyed earth." He feels "natural" and at peace.[58]

In the dream, transcendence has reconciled itself with the force of gravity and union with the inanimate. Male and female principles are united; spirit and matter, creation and destruction are seen as integral to the whole in a kind of Jungian mandala of personality integration.

Though the earth reclaims both the rocket and the rainbow, it is a wet-valleyed earth that does so; that is, it is a fertile earth that once again will give rise to consciousness and to the transcendental quest, just as the double-integral-shaped tunnels of Peenemunde brought forth the rocket to its launch at the holy center.[59] The impulse to transcendence is in the earth, in the so-called inanimate. It is replicated in the procreation of living creatures, and in their transformation of inanimate substances into further power-formations, ramifying systems which they control and use to their own ends of securing and enlarging themselves.

The impulse to transcendence which creates gravity's rainbow is part of V., the elemental force for change, creation, and destruction that is basic to consciousness, to the universe, fundamental to the nature of our closed system. To think that it will take us out of our system is perhaps one of its qualities, one of its *charms.* (The particle physicists use that term to define an inexplicable attraction.)

What occurs in the drive to transcendence is explained metaphorically in the rocket's development, placement, firing, and trajectory. The rocket is born of an ideal that is systematically linked to earlier stages of technological development in plastics, fuels, metallurgy, engineering, ballistics, and so forth for its realization. It is a culmination of developments that seem in retrospect to have been inevitably going on to produce the rocket's rainbow flight. It is placed for firing as nations have been placed geographically, with certain resources at their disposal, and its site determines its proposed trajectory and *Brennschluss*. *Brennschluss* is the point at which the rocket's fuel is cut off, determined in the rocket by a building charge, which may be construed as the desire for transcendence, that finally equals a preset charge, or a psychological threshold or energy limit, and closes a switch. At that point the rocket is on its own, subject to its own momentum and the force of gravity (conscious desire has ceased), heading toward a predetermined point of contact, which in the case of the V-2 was merely a grid of probabilities, not an exact point of contact. (Even today's long-range missiles are subject to in-flight variables that are too numerous to calculate and compensate for exactly.)

Pynchon describes *Brennschluss* as a point of integration, a point without motion. It is also a point of interface, when one system closes out to be succeeded by another, the rocket in one split second moved by its own energy and in the next controlled by gravity. *Brennschluss,* like the moment of completed ejaculation, marks the point at which the motion toward the transcendent ideal, ceases, and the unconscious, but governing forces of the universe take over. There is a zero point that is reached in our spiritual, imaginative flight, and from there the trajectory is downward to an opposite zero point and to an integration with the still fertile inanimate. The proper geometric representation is parabolic, possibly circular, a rainbow over a valley, possibly a benzene ring, or the Oriental snake with mouth to tail.[60]

The zero points and the variability of aim points are important to Pynchon as they are scientific assurance that science cannot wholly do away with the possibilities of transfer to new systems and with the element of surprise. Pynchon also spends a good deal of time in *Gravity's Rainbow* elevating Werner Heisenberg's principle of indeterminancy, which states the impossibility of measuring exactly the whereabouts of subatomic particles, to a kind of God's grace that assures us that man can never so completely control the outcome of events as to make his system into a kind of Skinnerian Walden Two or into Pointsman's fully conditioned Pavlovian state.

There is at the heart of Pynchon's view of our late twentieth-century situation a very pure and old-fashioned romanticism that extols the basic goodness of individual spontaneity and human instinct. Human evil can be laid to severe repression of the instincts instead of their proper recognition and sympathetic education. Blacks and Orientals have not developed out of the ascetic traditions of Western Christianity and are, therefore, kinder, more sympathetic, and more accepting of life. The innocent will survive because he is in tune with his instincts and has a kind of animal grace that the intellectual system builders and controllers lack.

Although Pynchon sees a kind of Hegelian inevitability in the historical movement from traditional religion to mysticized technology, he obviously does not like or trust the concept of historical inevitability. It is the moments of interface that really interest him and offer hope, for these are the moments of possibility for change, for transfer. History is, he would have us believe, discontinuous, reaching its various zero points, a balance of opposing forces, only to move into a new phase quite different from the last, a phase that is not really very predictable at all. There is a sort of despairing hope that our present phase is running itself out at last, as Pynchon's transcendental industrialist Lyle Bland suggests, and that we may yet become antitechnological, individualistic, instinctive, and loving. In Leo Marx's terms, Pynchon wants the machine out of the garden, and, like all good New England Transcendentalists, he would prefer a society centered around Walden One.

Chapter 2
Method in the Madness

Although Pynchon's novels are basically novels of quest on the part of a central character and his associates and as such may be to some degree identified with the old-fashioned Grail quest romances of Arthurian legend, his knights-errant are not heroic. The "heroism" is ridiculous, and they are affected more by circumstances than by any talents of their own. Their amoral world teaches them no clear-cut moral lessons. They feel keenly a loss of personal freedom and an estrangement from organized human activity that makes them cynical, analytical, paranoid, and determined to persevere on their own terms nevertheless. They do persevere since they keep faith in a kinder, freer world; they oppose the disillusioning reality with a vision of their own, half analysis and half dream.

With Pynchon we are always in the mind of the author. Characters are spokesmen for his viewpoints, and the mode of thought shifts readily but not always easily from a narrative explanation to a rush of associative imagery and back again, so that for the reader the transition is often difficult to follow. Pynchon is also not one to throw anything away. There are many parts of his novels, particularly *Gravity's Rainbow,* that appear to be interpolated pieces of early apprentice work. The childish writing of the Byron the Bulb parable in *Gravity's Rainbow* and the SHROUD and SHOCK colloquy in *V.* are examples. The doggerel that dots the pages of *Gravity's Rainbow,* though probably meant to spoof the idea of lyricism in our less than lyrical age, is so ham-handed it is not even humorous.

Structurally, *V.* is disjointed and discordant and so is *Gravity's Rainbow,* but one cannot deny Pynchon's remarkable gift for words. In Pynchon the poetry is in the prose, and there is an enormous amount of it in his last novel. It is also in the language that we find the method, the order, of the writing. It is language in the highest Puritan tradition, for in the language is the Word and the Image of our most divine quality—Thought. Cotton Mather punned his way through his homilies concerning the divine operations of Providence in Massachusetts. Jonathan Edwards looked for correspondence between the operations of spiders and worms and the workings of God. Edward Taylor did the same in his poetry and also made elaborate metaphors out of the artifacts of technology of his own age, spinning wheels and looms. Pynchon carries on the tradition of correspondences, metaphors, and signs in his quest for an organizing principle in the chaos of sensations and circumstances that our faster-paced century projects.

It should be noted too that although Pynchon's use of language and search for signs within it has respectable Puritan antecedents in his own ancestral past, it is far from being an old-fashioned exercise. Practitioners of the *Nouveau Roman* such as Alain Robbe-Grillet and Claude Simon exert themselves within more severe limits in the same direction. Roland Barthes, the chief theoretician of the New Novel has gone so far as to say that language is reality, for it is language that gives us the relation of things to their signs (words) and of the signs to each other, the structure of our world as we think it. In his later work, *Mythologie,* though, Barthes finds that signs can be other than words and, therefore, that language is only one means of discovering the relationship of things and systems of things.[61]

In Robbe-Grillet's *dans le labyrinthe* there is a constant circling about through the memory of the narrator that results in an excavation of signs and war and relgion, but, unlike Pynchon, Robbe-Grillet does not give us an explication. The author hesitates and then moves on. The signs stand on their own, referred to again in different contexts, but not explained. Where the French materialist refuses to go beyond the evocation of signs, the Puritan idealist must shower the sign with language that explores and details its relational aspects, to give it some definite possibilities of meaning. For Robbe-Grillet such an effort would merely encourage a dangerous belief in an elaborate mental construct which is only illusion, a trick of the mind. Both authors mistrust systematic thought, but Pynchon cannot leave it alone any more than Oedipa Maas or Slothrop can.

Pynchon's approach is the more thorough. Robbe-Grillet seems more concerned with how signs are evoked than what their ramifications are. Writing is an exploration of the arousal of thought for the New Novelist. For Pynchon writing is an exploration of the connections of the thought-stuff that has already been aroused from the Unconscious.

The attitude toward metaphors is also at opposite extremes in Robbe-Grillet and Pynchon. Robbe-Grillet says that the metaphor is never "innocent"; that is, it always suggests a kind of spiritual unity in the universe which is not there. Robbe-Grillet's use of signs, however, is in the last analysis metaphoric, for a sign must stand for something, and, whether it is explicated or not in the text, the second the reader recognizes it as a sign or symbol the metaphoric connection is made. Pynchon, of course, uses metaphors precisely for the purpose of finding unity, just as Taylor, and Mather and Edwards did before him. Pynchon shares the concern over the function of metaphors of the linguistically oriented writers of the *Nouveau Roman* and theoreticians of the *Tel Quel* group gathered about Philippe Sollers. He knows that metaphors can mislead, that they can be dictatorial, and that their meanings must always be considered tentative, changing, and incomplete. He uses metaphors unabashedly, however, for they are a natural method of thinking, and without them the possibilities of the imagination and, indeed, of intellectual comprehension are enormously reduced.

Gravity's Rainbow not only contains a titular metaphor that encapsules the meaning of this very long book, but the narrative is enclosed at the beginning and at the end in metaphors. The book opens with Pirate Prentice's nightmare of the falling V-2, the evacuation of London, and the question of salvation as people wait huddled together in the black of night. The book ends, as we all know, with Blicero's rocket streaming down over a congregation of people in the movie house, still hoping for salvation.

Some major currents of metaphors that serve as organizing motifs in this most metaphoric of all his novels are: (1) those of chance and probability, such as Slothrop's sex chart, the Casino Hermann Goering, and the fortune-teller's tarot pack; (2) those of religion and spiritual quest such as the rocket and its rainbow, the use of spiritual mediums and communications with the dead in the case of Lyle Bland and Nora Dodson Truck, the walk of Enzian and Christian, references to the Hanged God, and light and dark imagery; (3) those of sex and creativity such as the double integral sign and the sign of the rocket, the rocket itself, and the archetypes of man and woman in male and femal characters; and (4) those of choice and change, such as the various "crossroads," "zero points," "interfaces," and "transfers."

The chief structural metaphor that rationalizes the discontinuity of the novel is that of the motion picture film. There are numerous fade-outs, abrupt scene changes, and close-ups, often tagged as such within the text. Sections of the novel are set off by a square hole symbol as though to suggest the sprocket hole of the motion picture film. We have a sense of frames being shot and cut, edited, and refitted as the author sees fit. But it would be wrong to suggest that the entire novel is presented in this mode, for there is much off-camera discourse and sections where the idea of a film presentation seems very much left behind.

The film metaphor is important thematically, though, as well as structurally. The media has conditioned many of the characters. The director Springer cannot really see the difference between how a person is treated in a motion picture and in real life. Pökler is dependent on pornographic films for his lovemaking. Von Göel produces, and Springer directs, a propaganda film on the *Schwartzkommando,* using people in the White Visitation in blackface as actors. Later, when he discovers that there really are *Schwartzkommando,* Springer thinks he invented them. Slothrop's life and loves keep "reeling" in circles from one Katje-like female to the next, as though he too were incapable of relating to more than a film stereotype. In his use of films Pynchon suggests that our technologized society has decreased the dimensions of our perception, flattened out our world, limited its communication, and caused a loss of human feeling, of real affect.

Among those critics dealing with Pynchon's use of films, Lane Roth has noted that Pynchon uses American musicals to suggest American innocence and hopefulness while using Fritz Lang's German films to show the politics of technological control, personal power, and death.[62] John Stark believes Pynchon is greatly indebted to German expressionist films such as Fritz Lang's *Dr. Mabuse* and the earlier *The Cabinet of Dr. Caligari* (1920), particularly in his use of setting with its many lines, sharp angles, and the use of light and shadow to develop a sense of uneasiness and fear.[63] Stark also notes that Siegfried Kracauer, in his book *From Caligari to Hitler*, "points out the suggestion frequently made by those films that the only political alternatives are tyranny and anarchy, the political analogues of paranoia and anitparanoia."[64] Pynchon's dialectical view of history was well served by the German films; moreover, so was Pynchon's theme of operational paranoia. In Fritz Lang's *The Spy* (1928), "no character was what he appeared to be. This constant change of identities was appropriate to denote a state of mind in which the paralysis of self interfered with any attempt at self-identification" (like Slothrop's change of identities and sense of a disintegrating self). The climax of the film occurred with a train wreck in a tunnel, the impression of which was given "through confused mental images of the persons involved in this shock situation."[65] The same effect is created when Slothrop experiences a train wreck in a tunnel near Nordhausen as he is being pursued by Major Marvy, who is under Pointsman's orders to recapture Slothrop.[66]

In dealing with a chaotic universe in which the individual has little sense of assured worth and where his will is almost unconsciously captive to the forces that will destroy him, Pynchon's method is that of the transcendental romantic. Like Samuel Taylor Coleridge and Emerson he finds the imagination a formative faculy, a means of constructing a suitable reality for the self out of contrary elements of the phenomenal world. Also, like Coleridge he finds a value in the free flow of associations as a kind of heuristic prelude to the gathering together and unifying process of the imagination. The formative power of the imagination is shown clearly in the way he centralizes the events of the novel around the rocket, the central metaphor, upon which all motifs of religion, sex, creativity, chance, and choice depend. The role of fancy is manifested in part by the associated but disconnected sections of the novel, the bad lyrics, the interpolated material, the shifts in viewpoint, the author's editorializing, and direct remarks to his own characters. It is, moreover, evidenced in the "play" of characters in the novel.

From Herbert Stencil forward it is customary for Pynchon's central characters to indulge in roleplaying as a means of finding out what experience has to offer in their search for a place and purpose in their lives. Stencil is a croupier in southern France and a plantation foreman in East Africa prior to his involvement in the quest for the V. of his father's letters. And in reading them, he "projects" the lives of those persons his father mentions, so that they become "Stencilized." Oedipa Maas falls into situations that make her react to the games of seduction, anarchic dance, and drama scholarship of others. She also plays her own game in a quest for what may be nothing more than a chimera of her own imagining. Tyrone Slothrop is the most energetic roleplayer of them all. As Rocketman and the fleeing Preterite pig he has molded his character on comic book heroes in a desperate attempt to attain salvation through a kind of chutzpah pride and then through self-effacing humility.

Slothrop's roles are also generally in accord with the traditional knight's quest for perfect virture. He learns the limits of pride and humility in these guises as he earlier learned the limits of courage, the value of temperance, and meaning of love in his exploits aboard the *Anubis,* his narrow escape at Putzi's, and his meetings with Bianca, Katje, and Solange, and as he finally experiences the *caritas* of one of the humble but persevering, the unmasked "pig" Pig Bodine, who brings the knight out of his despair.

The fantasies of the characters protect them against a systemized world ruled by an unfeeling, anonymous Them. When Oedipa becomes worried about her loss of contact with reality, her psychiatrist, Dr. Hilarius, tells her to cherish her fantasy, for to relinquish it is to go over to the "others."[67] Johan Huizinga, the sociologist, tells us that fantasies are the "discharge of superabundant energy,... satisfaction of 'imitative instinct.'" Also, according to others, it is "an outlet for harmful impulses, an acting out of wish-fulfillment," and "a fiction designed to keep up the feeling of personal value."[68]

The British writer Siegfried Sassoon and others who have been wounded in war and pretty well shell-shocked, speak of acting roles, of a divided self acting differently to different audiences and even to themselves, being both actor and detached observer. This sort of playacting about the awful *nada,* as Hemingway calls the nothingness at the center of one's existence, made suddenly starkly *there* for the perceiving self, seems to be a way of trying to create some sort of believable, wish-fulfilling reality to counteract the knowledge of *nada* and to affirm it through reference to an outside audience of believers in life, to reestablish one's need-fulfillment ties with other beings, real or imaginary. Rats became the audience for trenchsoldiers on watch in World War I, and soldiers seriously wounded often had the sense of standing outside themselves wondering if the poor blighter would make it.[69]

Whether we are listening to Nick Adams in Hemingway's "A Way You'll Never Be," filling his void with words as a way of turning off the terror, or watching Slothrop tearing around in a cape as Rocketman or in a pig costume like a comic book character playing to an audience of innocents, we are in fact witnessing the same use of fantasies to change the nature of a life-threatening reality.

When the order of things appears too threatening and there is no logical means of counteracting it, then the ego resorts to the illogical and the fanciful. In order to minimize the threat of German rockets, the characters call them "incoming mail." In order to trivialize Major Marvy's threat to Slothrop, so that Slothrop can still function in a threatening environment where he really has no power, Slothrop, while airborne in a balloon, engages Marvy in a pie-throwing contest and loses his pursuer in the clouds. Marvy is treated throughout like the comic book villain who must eventually be defeated for no other reason than that he is the villain and that good must triumph over evil. We do not believe in Marvy, but we do recognize him, for we have seen him in countless Disney cartoons, such as the cat in Mighty Mouse, and the wolf in Porky Pig.

If one's personality has been conditioned by the system, one is then, playing the role that has been set by the "others" that Oedipa has come to fear, and that Slothrop does his best to escape. Sent off on an obsessive search for the *Schwartzgerät* by Allied Intelligence, Slothrop begins to question the whole proposition. Enzian tells him that the name *Schwartzgerät* need not signify any reality, though Enzian himself appears to be searching for the instrument and its prototypical 0000 rocket. He is also told that the Americans, British, and Russians appear to be ready to mount an offensive against Enzian's Herreros. Pynchon tells his hero Slothrop that he is on someone else's trip and asks him where the Pope's staff is that is supposed to bloom for this foolish Tannhauser. Immediately thereafter, Slothrop dons the remnants of a Wagnerian opera costume and becomes Racketmensch. He is christened in his new role by the counterfeiter and dope dealer Saüre Bummer and is ready to play his own game.[70]

Ineffective in fact, one can triumph in fancy. In *V.* when Benny Profane worries about being in the grip of the inanimate, he gets drunk, and at sundown he pisses at the sun trying to think that he is putting it fire out.[71] In *Gravity's Rainbow* when Roger Mexico learns that Slothrop has been followed since before the war and thinks Pointsman to blame, he enters a corporate directors meeting and pisses on all present except Pointsman, for whom he has nothing left. Vowing to track him down, Mexico seizes a faceless steel magnate by his cock or his tie, "whichever is handier" (Pynchon here is stage directing). Mexico uses the magnate as a hostage and makes his escape. Mexico thus takes on the fleeing lover of the Preterite role from Slothrop, who has by this time in the novel had his conflict-resolving rainbow cock dream.[72]

As Pirate Prentice has said, those who are victimized by the system have the power of disorder, or irrationality. This power seems anarchic and destructive, but its playfulness is heuristic. It does open up possibilities that might not have been accessible through ordered thought. The indulgence of novelists of the Absurd in fantasies seemingly for their own sake, as we often see it in Pynchon, Barth, and Vonnegut, and as we sometimes see it in Existential quest novels by Bellow, Ellison, and Mailer, seems to be a way of getting beyond our rational understanding of things to see what meaning unstructured, unlooked-for experience might serendipitously bring. It is through his use of disguise and roleplaying that Slothrop discovers the balance of world forces that are emblemized in the rainbow cock dream.

In his essay "The Stylization of Desire" William Gass makes the point that desire becomes extended in a complicated means to an end that is sometimes forgotten. This is what happens historically in the development of ritual and process in such activities as banqueting, courtship, and art. Throughout the older civilizations there was a constant building up and tearing down of these forms of complicated foreplay, delayed gratification, and intensification and extension of pleasure.[73] Pynchon's novels, *V., The Crying of Lot 49,* and *Gravity's Rainbow,* are all about desire, as may be seen in the various forms of V., in Oedipa's quest for the Trystero, and in *Gravity's Rainbow* in the ritualized rocketry of Blicero, and in the sadomasochism of the guilty and destructive Pökler, Weissman (Blicero), Katje, and Slothrop. Pynchon's work is a sociological projection of the twentieth century's stylization of desire; that is, Pynchon is presenting to us in the random activity of his characters, the "foreplay" of our time, the artifacts and artifices by which we hope to gain a vaguely envisioned consumation.

A final aspect of play in Pynchon's work is wordplay. He is not nearly so involved and adroit in this respect as William Gass or those international linguists Nabokov and Jorge Luis Borges, but in one respect he has no competition—in the art of names.

To name a thing is to relate it to other things and classes of things, to give it an operable reality in the human mind. In primitive societies the act of naming as curse or blessing was a means of engaging the force of one's will for or against the object and was believed to actually have physical effect where ordinary physical means were impotent. Certainly, naming an object alters perception, for once a thing is named, it is inevitably thought of in certain associative contexts. These contexts expand and shape the reality of a thing beyond the immediate sensation of the object; they also limit the way in which the object can be considered.

The associations connected with a name are associations both of sound—of similar-sounding words and parts of words, and also of similar-sounding experiences—and of word structure, that is, of similar word roots, inflections, spellings, and anagrammatic combinations. In primitive societies sympathetic magic may utilize one object to affect a quite different object of similar name, as though the similarity of name meant a psychic connection that could be tapped and made to operate according to the will of the sorcerer. To find the right word, then, to describe a thing, to name it, is to exert power over it through a definition of contexts in which it can be considered and by the insinuation of its relatedness to unlikely things less readily apprehended and controlled.

Mark Siegel has observed that Pynchon recognizes the possibilities and limits of names in *Gravity's Rainbow.* In that book, Enzian notes, "There may be not gods, but there is a pattern: names by themselves may have no magic, but the *act* of naming, the physical utterance, obeys the pattern." The "pattern" is the relational necessity that forms human consciousness. Putting life into language, however, is also to institutionalize it and to destroy the primitive, immediate, more "true" responses to human life, as Tchitcherine threatens to destroy the primitive Khirghiz culture with the introduction of an alphabet.[74] The fascination with words can remove one from a feeling response to physical events. This is the case with Stephen Dodson-Truck, who knows thirty-three languages and is a supreme observer of life and reporter of its activities, but who is quite unable to keep his wife Nora satisfied sexually.[75]

Should the name have a context that is too confining, one can rename. Thus Weissman takes an SS code name, Dominus Blicero, from the German word *Blicker,* the nickname the early Germans gave to "Death." They saw Death as white, bleaching to blankness, which is in keeping with Weissman's original name, white man. Blicero is the white man, master of death, the knowing man *(Ich weiss,* "I know"), the man of science, and seeker after a unified "bliss" *(Blic-)* at the "zero" *(-cero)* point in the trajectory of a rocket manufactured at such sites as Bleicheerode, a name that Enzian connects with Blicker.[76] Thus, like Fitzgerald's Gatsby, with a change of name the white man proposes his destiny.

Names lead to a trail of associations that can be followed name to name, as it is in *V.* The associations do have a common denominator, a common associative factor in this case, which is the libidinous impulse, V. Midway through the novel Stencil speculates that in hunting for V. through its various characterizations he may end up "face-to-face with himself afflicted by a kind of soul-transvestism."[77] There is V. in Stencil too, and the various personalities of V. which he V-names are, after all, his own projections into the data of his father's letters.

The V-names all have V. as a common denominator, and beyond V. one annot go. Stencil says that the relations of Victoria to Veronica and the Vheissu plot suggest a historical trend, active today, an ultimate Plot Which Has No Name.[78] God has an ineffable name in the Old Testament, and the Absurdist Samuel Beckett's source of man's consciousness is the Unnamable. We cannot know the quintessence of our existence in terms of language and its associative qualities. Language is restrictive. Naming comes to an end.

The quest for an all-encompassing Principle that can be encapsuled in a name leads either to a sense of things as totally Other, the I insignificant and subject to forces ineffably larger than itself, or back into solipsism where the I is the definer of all that is. Stencil's fear that his quest may lead to the discovery that he is "afflicted with a kind of soul-transvestism" suggests that he recognizes the solipsistic nature of knowing, that all he does know is bounded by his own perception of things conditioned by his own desires. The same is true of Slothrop in *Gravity's Rainbow* when in a dream he discovers that his foster father's name Jamf means "I."[79] Slothrop's psychoanalyst tells him that Jamf is his own invention, a personification of his own projected guilt. Yet, Jamf can also be looked upon as the necessary evil in a Mannichaean universe, and as a part of himself, of Tyrone Slothrop, as a representative part or microcosm of that universe. Names in both of these novels become a way of expressing the paradoxical nature of consciousness; that is, that the perceiver "contains" what he perceives and yet that he does not fully control it.

Names not only involve words but signs as well. In *The Crying of Lot 49* the muted post horn emblem serves as a "name." It is a symbol for a rebel postal system and more generally for antiinstitutionalism and for free communication of thought and feeling. Oedipa's search for the lost word, "the cry that might abolish the night," results only in the finding of such "signs," which she regards as a "kind of compensation" for the loss of innocence and its protective authority, the father or mother who could "abolish the night" for the frightened child.[80]

In *Gravity's Rainbow* signs ramify in meaning and suture together views of sex, love, creativity, science and religion. Two of the most important signs are the double integral $\int\int$ and the symbol of the rocket . The double integral is the shape of the rocket tunnels at Peenemunde, and the sign also suggests the shape of lovers copulating. The double integral is a mathematical sign that indicates completion and wholeness created out of variable parts. The sign then is one that unifies the libidinous impulse with that of human creativity and a transcendent desire for oneness. The rocket suggests the "holy center" (man's idealizing consciousness) from which it is fired and the burning energy within its unified structure. The fins have an obvious reference in Slothrop's mind to the cross, now technologized. The author finds in the shape of things the shape of man's deepest fears and desires.

In addition to the names and signs there are also certain words that suggest far more than their specified meanings as technical terms. As indicated earlier, the rocket terms "Brennschluss" and *zero point,* for example, operate in connection with the rhythms of desire, history, and consciousness. *Preterite* too is a term that goes far beyond its Calvinist theological application. In Calvinist terms it refers to those who are not of the elect, those who have been passed over and have no future in heaven. In grammatical terms Roland Barthes tells us, "Through the Preterite [my capitalization], the verb implicitly belongs with a causal chain; it partakes of a set of related and oriented actions; it functions as the algebraic sign of an intention." He goes on to say that it is the narrative tense, and lurking behind it is a Creator, God, or Demiurge.[81] So, grammatically, "Preterite" refers to those people, things, and events that are past as part of a determined chain of events. Theologically and grammatically Preterition is a mode of thought that models itself on the past. In both the theological and grammatical meanings of the term future possibility is forsworn. To open up a new and promising mode of thought, one has to break with the Preterite and think in the present. The predominant tense in which Pynchon's characters "play" out their possibilities is the rushing present.

Pynchon's frequent expressions of doubt as to the truth of what his characters perceive, his way of showing their perception in various modes, such as that of film projection and free-association, and of putting them in various guises, places, and lights are all methods of lightening the heavy hand of the past and restoring the elements of possibility. Add to these effects Pynchon's various transition devices such as the "crossroads" and "zero points" as well as his discussions of scientific uncertainty in terms of statistics and particle physics and it is easy to see Pynchon, child of the Puritans and Weberian Calvinist dropout, striking a blow on behalf of the Preterite against Determinism and Preterition, for Possibility.

Nevertheless, Pynchon's work remains darkly comic. The hero seems all too ineffectual, the rocket all too menacing, and although Rocketman's roleplaying offers a kind of psychic escape, it offers no adequate counterforce against the serious threat of obliterating technological death. Enzian's Christianity is seemingly too blind and too weak to be a true counterforce. We are not ready for the kind of Taoist acceptance signified by Slothrop's rainbow cock dream, and the only alternative mockingly offered is that we join in singing an antiquated hymn.

The reader's response to Pynchon's dark comedy is the laughter of recognition, a release of pent-up tension in a forced confession of his own divided need for freedom and order, a release of the tension built up by his denial of the futility of trying to reconcile the two goals. His laughter can easily give way to despair if he should see the absurdity as more than partial, temporary, or of limited consequence to his desires.

Chapter 3
The Novelist as Remorseful Absurdist

With his recent novel, *Jailbird*, Kurt Vonnegut dropped the "Jr." from the end of his name, a sign that he feels he has come into his own. Certainly, with his popularity among the college generation of the 1960s and increasing critical acclaim in the 1970s, he has every right to view himself in that light.

At first, his appeal to the young was considered by serious critics as merely a sign of his own puerility, but they have gradually recognized that Vonnegut is constantly dealing with basic philosophical questions, and he is not always offering simplistic answers. He is nevertheless, admittedly sentimental, and that has put off more than one critic. The sentimentality, however, is this sensitive author's emotional reaction to his intellectual apprehension of a world inescapably absurd.

Vonnegut, who studied originally in the sciences, has, like others so educated, Pynchon and Mailer for example, found our technology an organizing metaphor for man's creative urge. His first novel, *Player Piano* (1952), takes the development of a technocracy to its logical conclusion; that is, rule of the elite (managers and engineers), displacement of workers by machines, conversion of nature to the uses of technology, and a gradual stifling of spontaneity and imagination, with the inevitable revolt by those who still have a need for their expression. In fact, he carries the course of events one step further, as the rebels begin reconstructing the very machines that have taken away their freedom. It is this cycle of evolution and dissolution, movement toward order and efficiency peaking and then collapsing toward anarchy and spontaneity, only to repeat once again, that is basic to Vonnegut's historical view. And it is what keeps him from offering any utopian correction or being morally indignant with his wrong-minded characters.

What many young readers in the 1960s failed to see in Vonnegut was that he was not only pointing out harmful social behavior in their middle-class elders, but that he was not offering any real hope that the paramount forces of behavior could be changed. These forces stem from basic qualities of human nature which are rooted in us, young and old alike. The best he could do was to sugarcoat the pill. The young college students and many of their young instructors swallowed it, loved the taste, and may now wonder why instead of the soothing charity of Eliot Rosewater they hear instead the tired conscience of Walter Starbuck in *Jailbird*.

The critic Clark Mayo is right when he notes that Vonnegut's Paul Proteus is a manipulated messiah figure who inadvertently not only satirizes the rewards of the Protestant work ethic but also the forms of old religions and the failure of new ones (like the Ghost Shirt Society) to replace them.[1] Paul recognizes the inevitable failure of reform with his toast at the end of the novel, "To the record," which is like the "So it goes" of *Slaughterhouse-Five*, and the "Hi ho" of *Player Piano* itself.

Vonnegut's second novel, *The Sirens of Titan* (1959), contends with the religious paradox of God as omniscient, omnipotent, and beneficient.

God, in this case, is the deceased millionaire Winston Niles Rumfoord. Life is, he knows, just one of the manifestations of the universe's chaotic becoming. Rumfoord is in the same situation as the later Billy Pilgrim in that he knows all that will happen but cannot change any of it, but, more heroically than Pilgrim, he will try. He builds up an army of programmed humans on Mars whose mission is to invade Earth to help him systematize human behavior and to make men happy. "The triumph of anything," he says, "is a matter of organization."

The invasion repulsed, Rumfoord sends a messiah, Malachi Constant, programmed with a message. He arrives in an orange suit with a question mark on it, a savior of doubt, bearing the name Unk, presumably for "Unknown." Unk is quickly shown to be a very fallible messiah, the unwitting murderer of his best friend, but he is forgiven and allowed to go aboard a spaceship bound for Titan, to join his beloved Beatrice and the child Chronos. Rumfoord's pastor offers a prayer to a God of apathy who has freed man from belief, making him "free, truthful, and dignified at last." Where God is indifferent to man's needs, where He makes him the sport of cosmic games, He cannot hold man accountable for his actions.

God in this case is governed by the laws of chance. He is neither omnipotent nor particularly beneficient, having sacrificed an army of hijacked earthlings to make unsuccessful war on their brethren. He may be omniscient, but it does Him and the humans made in His image no good.

An alternative to engineering human happiness or to a reliance on divine revelation is to encourage a life of "hypnotic anarchy," such as that now led on the robot space traveler Salo's home planet. It is a way of life that has supposedly endured for 620,000 earthling years. On that planet creatures once sought a higher purpose, but no purpose was high enough. They also sought greater efficiency and turned over their labors to the machines. The machines caused the creatures to destroy themselves because the machines found them purposeless.

Salo's role in the anarchic scheme is to travel in his spaceship around the universe with a piece of metal that has a single dot on it that is supposed to translate as "Greetings!" Vonnegut saw our nation's space ventures as a kind of reaching out for contact with superior intelligence, a reaching for God. The human space explorers, however, found that "the boundaries of space, of infinite outwardness, were three: empty heroics, low comedy, and pointless death."[2] Salo's mission is no less pointless.

The failure of purpose in religion and technology in a universe whose only order is a kind of "hypnotic anarchy" is also the subject of *Cat's Cradle* (1963), and the problem of moral responsibility for operating in an absurd universe is the unsettling theme of *Mother Night* (1961).

Of the two, *Cat's Cradle* is closer in statement and treatment to *The Sirens of Titan*. The man of science is the inventor of *ice-nine*, a compound designed to freeze mud so that soldiers will not have to march through the sticky stuff. It also freezes anything else it comes in contact with. Felix Hoenikker is the quintessentially curious scientist. He loves toys, and the play of his own imagination is his primary concern. The social effects of his tinkering with nature's laws are of little consequence to him. He is also one of the fathers of the atomic bomb. Vonnegut's own father, who was oblivious to headlines and questions of social justice, interested himself almost exclusively in materials and architecture and appears to be the prototype.[3]

The altruistic Julian Castle presents an alternative to the way of science and technology. He leads a kind of Albert Schweitzer life in the jungle, giving his all against human misery, until the end. When Hoenikker's son Newt shows him a painting he calls "Cat's Cradle," with all its meaningless crosses, Castle throws it off the terrace, proclaiming that it is as impossible to know if there is no meaning in the world as it is to know if there is. God gets the benefit of the doubt in this view.

Bokonon, the shipwrecked black sailor turned holy man, believes man alone is sacred. He would die thumbing his nose at You Know Who. He and Corporal McCabe, the other shipwrecked visitor to the poor island of San Lorenzo, try to set up a society based on communism and find the people so poor that the divided wealth comes to six and seven dollars a share per adult. The capitalists of the Castle Sugar Company failed to make much out of San Lorenzo and so do McCabe and Bokonon, but Bokonon's harmless lies, his "foma," do help people to deal with their misery, as religions do.

The president of the island "republic," Papa Monzano, has outlawed Bokonon and his religion, but when he is dying, he wants the last rites of Bokonon. The opposition of political and religious authorities is necessary, a "dynamic tension" that keeps the organism of the state in good health. Bokonon must always be hunted but never killed, for the populace would then ask for all the comforts of paradise, and the republic is too poor to support them. So the rites of Bokonon go on in contravention of the authority that knows they must go on for it to survive. And Bokonon knows too that he only appears good because Papa Monzano seems so evil. His self-awareness is borne out when he leads the survivors of a catastrophic air show to mass suicide in the bowl of Mount McCabe. Mona, the beautiful, literally all-loving, presumably virginal, adopted daughter of Papa Monzano happily goes to her death in this way.

John, the narrator of this book, calls himself Jonah, and in at least one way this is Vonnegut's book of Jonah, as his critic Richard Giannone has pointed out.[4] Jonah is a quester after moral purpose, and finds none. He finds that the scientists and industrialists honestly believe that they are on earth to make things and believe that life will be better for it, that religion is only a palliative at best and the handmaiden of oppression at its worst, that art but mirrors reality, and that love in its purest, ideal form is nihilistic, and otherwise only a temporary expedient. After the destruction of Papa's castle, the wife of the industrialist, Crosby, knits in the rubble an American flag, and Jonah thinks, American that he is, that he is destined to plant it atop Mount McCabe. If there is a purpose, it seems to be, symbolically, if no other way, for the American to set himself atop the worthless island and its bowl of suicides. The way of Bokonon may be preferable after all.

At the air show featuring the six planes of the San Lorenzan Air Force, Ambassador Minton speaks of the stupidity and viciousness of mankind and mourns openly the loss of a son in war (World War II) that he says was fought by children. Prior to that Felix's son, Frank Hoenikker, who has bought himself a job with Papa Monzano by giving him a vial of *ice-nine*, sees Papa in rigid death, and his only statement is that the mess must be cleaned up. Jonah (Vonnegut) sees Frank's comment as the typical response of the technocrat to the immoral destruction his technology has caused. The elements present at the novel's close—the mindless patriotism of the Crosbys and Jonah himself, the reference to children's crusades that are fought for its causes, and the amoral rationalizations for technology misapplied for patriotic purposes—prefigure the themes of *Salughterhouse-Five* (1969).

While *Cat's Cradle* and *Slaughterhouse-Five* suggest a world of farce with their caricature characters and their pretentious buffoonery, *Mother Night* (1961), on the other hand, is a serious first-person, confessional novel, told by the playwright-turned-propagandist Howard W. Campbell about his activities as a spy. Occupational roleplaying and what the role does to one's moral judgment is a continuing concern in Vonnegut's work. In *Player Piano* Paul Proteus discovers that thinking in engineering terms has led the leaders to engineering human beings without concern for their deepest needs for autonomy, productive work, and resultant sense of self-worth. In *The Sirens of Titan* Winston Niles Rumfoord plays God and sacrifices humanity to save it from a belief in a traditional God who has failed. In *Cat's Cradle* the scientist plays with matter and invents new forms without concern for their social effects. In all the novels, success in the roles of political reformer, scientist, or saint leads to overplaying, going beyond the boundaries of the role, as the actor is corrupted by a sense of power. Moreover, the point at which one really is becoming corrupt may not be easily apprehended. We are all creatures of self-delusion. In *Mother Night* Howard C. Campbell seems to slip with terrible inevitability into the role of traitor.

Wirtanen, the American agent, who recruits him for his role as a spy broadcasting propaganda from Germany, plays on his sense of drama and lust for heroism. He is used by the Allies to send out coded messages that he himself does not understand, but his propaganda is so well delivered that Werner Noth, his father-in-law and a Nazi official, tells him that he does not really care if he is a spy; his broadcasts have been very effective for the Nazi cause and he has spoken ideas that were latent in Noth's own mind, confirming his own allegiance to Nazi Germany.

When confronted by his own countrymen as a traitor after the war, Campbell seeks the help of one of the few who knows his intended purpose in Germany, the man who recruited him, Wirtanen. Wirtanen says that if he testifies for him it will not be because he feels any guilt for Campbell's position. Campbell was a reprehensible figure during the war, after all, having played his role too well. Wirtanen testifies for him only because he loves the contest, the battle of wits. The master spy Wirtanen would be as much a manipulator of human beings for the sake of his own God-like satisfactions as was Winston Niles Rumfoord.

Even when his logic is terrible, people believe the propagandist because they want to believe him. Able to see his own situation, while broadcasting for the Germans, Campbell can only laugh as one caught in an absurd position.[5]

Against the world that accepted his satanic performance for his true self, he and Helga Noth, daughter of the police chief of Berlin, opposed a "nation of two."[6] After Helga's disappearance into a Russian concentration camp after the war and his marriage to Resi, Helga's sister, Resi describes Campbell as "used up." She says, "There is nothing left of him but curiosity and a pair of eyes."[7] Peter Reed, one of Vonnegut's critics, has pointed out that a "nation of two" cannot endure because although it provides mutual support it "also has elements of evasion, illusion, and egocentrism."[8] Man also has social needs that cannot be supplied by a loving partner alone, though she may help him to endure disappointing situations as the loyal and sympathetic Mrs. Minton does as the wife of the ambassador to San Lorenzo in *Cat's Cradle*.

Campbell is tracked down by a vengeful veteran, O'Hare. The former spy bests the avenger with the aid of a pair of fireplace tongs. Rightful avengers are as misguided as anyone else for their intolerance and twice as inexcusable in Vonnegut's view. So is the one who robs another of his profession. When the Russian who has stolen Campbell's plays and had them performed to his own credit in Russia seems on the pinnacle of success, it is discovered that he also wrote a travesty on the Red Army, and he is then shot.

Despite these little "triumphs," Campbell in the end is bereft of love, professional recognition, and, most awful of all, uncertain of his own integrity. Out of guilt, he asks a doctor neighbor, Dr. Epstein, to turn him over to the Israelis. Epstein wants nothing to do with such vengeance, though he spent his boyhood in Auschwitz. His mother, however, says that Campbell should have what he wants. She recognizes that he in his own cataleptic condition is not unlike the prisoners at Auschwitz who wanted some authority to speak for them. Mrs. Epstein is Mother Night, the intolerant authority who controls through guilt, whose rule makes a mockery of choice and leads us away to death.

Once again in this work we find a pernicious circle of events. The American lust for adventure and heroism is captured by the ideals of patriotism and made to serve its destructive ends. When the patriotism is seen as ambivalent, as symbolized by Campbell's attic window painting of swastika, hammer and sickle, and stars and stripes, the rationale for destruction fails, and the individual is overcome with guilt. Campbell's tragic flaw is his inability to see himself in perspective and to hold to that view. Assaulted on all sides by other people's perceptions of him, there is no authority he can turn to that will assure him that the role of an actor is in great measure conditioned by the director and by the expectations of his audience, that the guilt he finds in himself should really be the guilt of the fanatical true-believers who either praise or scorn him, represented by the American Nazis and the avenging O'Hare respectively. (This same idea is even more clearly pointed up in Vonnegut's later novel *Jailbird*.) Like Werner Noth, Campbell will hang, a symbolic hanged god, a sacrifice to man's ruined innocence. His recognition as such will probably be as dubious as Noth's, whose death is featured in a pornographic magazine, where the description of Noth hanging from a budding apple tree, his bare toes touching the ground, his penis erecting, is reminiscent of repetitive scenes in William Burroughs's surrealistic antiauthoritarian, antipropaganda novel, *Naked Lunch.*

Cast into uncertain roles, convinced of the legitimacy of those roles, we carry on according to the script, too often unquestioningly, our success blinding us to the evil of our actions. Werner Noth was the chief of police of Berlin, and he merely upheld the law, but his chiefs of prisons mistreated their prisoners. Eichmann is in an Israeli prison with Campbell and is more interested in selling his book than in saving his own life. Like Campbell he was looking for heroism and found it in an unsavory role legitimized by his own government. To the end, his role means more to him than life itself. Neither war criminal is castigated by Campbell, nor will Campbell flagellate himself, for he sees no alternative path. He feels guilty, though, without knowing the true source of his guilt. The entire tone of his confession is that of a man who is "used up," used up in the way that all devices are used up, programmed to perform in a certain way until their function is no longer needed, then displaced. The human "device" that is functionless in Western society is apt to feel guilty, particularly if his previous functions are denigrated. He becomes a candidate for suicide, as Campbell does.

The human being used by the system for immoral purposes often develops protective schizophrenia, refusing to make logical connections between his actions and evil effects. To do otherwise would threaten his sense of self-worth, alienate him from the system that has nurtured him, and cast him into that scary state of freedom and self-responsibilty that Dostoevski's Grand Inquisitor said made the Catholic Church inevitable. The villain of the piece is not Noth, Eichmann, or the comic American Nazi Dr. Lionel J.D. Jones, who is so schizophrenic that he has a black and a Catholic as faithful henchmen while he rails against both blacks and Catholics endlessly. The villain is an amoral authoritarian, technocratic state that uses the call of patriotism to make its citizens carry out the designs of its power elite. A representative form of government is no assurance against such authoritarianism. So long as men seek authority for their actions, the power elite will, of necessity, arise, and, seeking their own extension of control (political, religious, or scientific), they will continue the use and misuse of human beings.

In *God Bless You, Mr. Rosewater* (1965) Vonnegut creates a neurotic character who once again owes his neurosis to the course of history, of American history in particular, and his neurosis is at once more vital and more preposterous than that of Howard Campbell. Eliot Rosewater is the scion of the moralistic, conservative senator from Indiana, Lister Rosewater. He is also the president of the multimillion dollar Rosewater Foundation, founded by a post-Civil War Rosewater in the heyday of speculation and laissez-faire. The foundation funds were augmented by Rosewater marriage into the Rockefeller and DuPont family fortunes.

Eliot accidentally killed his mother in a sailing accident when he was nineteen. The mother is described by Eliot as wise and amusing with a genuine concern for the poor. She was quite unlike his father Lister Rosewater, who preaches laissez-faire capitalism and the justified damnation of the poor. Aware of his heritage on both sides, Eliot carries a double burden of guilt for having destroyed goodness and being the beneficiary of wealth wrung from the sweat of less fortunate people.

Alcoholic, bookish, and without close friends, Eliot easily mistakes illusion for reality, as in the scene where he commands from his box in the theater that the singers in the tomb in *Aida* not sing, so as to conserve oxygen. Fascinated by the innovative gadgetry of science, he believes that science will improve the world just as Felix Hoenniker, the inventor of *ice-nine* did, and he loves the science-fiction writers for dealing with the big questions. A guilty innocent with a desire to save the world, Eliot Rosewater is a familiar American type, at once admirable for his good heart and dangerous for his wrongheadedness.

Having killed three unarmed German firemen during the war when he was an army captain, Rosewater becomes fanatically attached to volunteer fire departments and begins one of his own in Rosewater County, Indiana. There he estalishes himself as the loving benefactor of the poor and the dispossessed.

Eliot's love, inspired as it is by guilt, is so generalized that he seldom remembers the names of those he has helped and who have in their lonely existence come to depend upon him. He is so schizophrenic that he can reduce an old housekeeper to tears when she rings up on the wrong phone and then treat her as a worthy foundation client when she immediately calls him back on the other, without making any connection in his own behavior as to the cause of her distress.

Eventually, he deserts those whom he has encouraged to feel dependent upon him, and as he is approaching Indianapolis, he has a vision of a firestorm destroying the city, a vision which for him is a purifying and holy image. In the insane asylum once again, Kilgore Trout assures him and his father that what he did in Rosewater County was not insane. "It was quite possibly the most important social experiment of our time, for it dealt on a very small scale with a problem whose queasy horrors will eventually be made worldwide by the sophistication of machines. The problem is this: how to love people who have no use?"[9] Vonnegut iterates a theme of *Player Piano*, and Eliot Rosewater's connection to the character of Paul Proteus becomes quite plain.

It is not poverty that is bad; it is uselessness. The system produces useless rich like the Buntlines and useless, poor hangers-on like Caroline Rosewater; the vacuity of their lives is about the same. Trout says that Eliot has shown the way by example as one who gave uncritical love over a long period of time. People without use will need all the uncritical love they can get.

Eliot's last act of uncritical love is to bestow the assets of the foundation on the fifty-seven children who people in Rosewater County say he fathered and to adjure them all to be fruitful and multiply. This shedding of responsibility on the young is more a curse than a blessing, an older generation's escape from the guilt it feels because of its ancestral past and a displacement of the burden of social responsibility on those who are all but unaware of the responsibilities of wealth and probably as unfit to manage it as the rich adults.

Eliot Rosewater is one of Vonnegut's ambiguous heroes, the one who most clearly embodies the ambiguities of the American Dream. American success is measured in material terms; money is the measure of our distinction, as the lawyer McCallister tells Stewart Buntline.[10] The makers of fortunes worked, fought, and connived; now their offspring feel guilty over the fighting and the conniving and know nothing of the work. A guilty social conscience demands appeasement in acts of indiscriminate giving, which, as the lawyer McCallister says, makes the poor neither rich nor comfortable. Having saved themselves, the rich would now save the world, on their own terms, as usual.

The subtitle of the book is "Pearls Before Swine." A Rosewater ancestor raised hogs. The rich slurp at the Money River. Eliot grows fat as a hog and lives like a pig in his dark, little office with its two telephones. Eliot's clients are, for the most part, self-pitying ne'er-do-wells and eccentrics like Diana Moon Glampers, the housekeeper, and Mary Moody, the firebug. The swine exist among the wealthy and poor alike. The title, *God Bless You, Mr. Rosewater,* which sounds like a benediction given to Eliot for his charitableness is given by the endlessly self-pitying Diana, and Eliot's insurance salesman cousin Fred Rosewater says that it has been applied to himself by grateful clients. He also uses this encomium as a part of a well-contrived sales pitch. One should not forget either that Kilgore Trout's rationalization for Eliot's behavior is given by a Jesus figure who has shaved off his beard and gone to work in a stamp redemption store. The benediction is mocked throughout. Eliot is not to be regarded as heroic, though many of Vonnegut's readers in the sixties saw him that way. His character is really the simplistic liberal counterpart to his father Lister's simplistic conservatism. Kilgore Trout, who is a kind of crackpot seer in Vonnegut's works, has nevertheless spoken the truth about man's need for use, and that is the very reason why Eliot's soppy, indiscriminate, guilt-inspired escape from purposeful employment, if it can be found, is at best a palliative for the hopeless ne'er-do-wells and definitely the wrong medicine for those capable of purposive employment, most of whom fled the embrace of Eliot's undiscriminating love and sought a life outside of Rosewater County.[11]

Capitalism and science appeared to many in the nineteenth century to be the appropriate means to human betterment. After two world wars, the bitter depression of the thirties, the advent of the atomic bomb and the missile race, and Asiatic wars in Korea and Vietnam, it became obvious that capitalism and science had created an enormous capacity for death and suffering. America's part in this development had become one of world leadership. The burden of responsibility for the effects were unmistakably ours.

Vonnegut had felt those effects directly in the Allied firebombing of Dresden, a supposedly unstrategic German city, while he was a prisoner of war there during World War II. Along with other POWs he was put to work burying the dead after this holocaust which incinerated hundreds of thousands of people, mostly German civilians. Donald J. Greiner has perceptively noted the similarity between Vonnegut's position as a survivor of Dresden and that of the survivors of Hiroshima. Robert J. Lifton studied the effects of the Hiroshima atom bomb on its Japanese survivors and found that they felt a great guilt at having survived while others in their community perished. It is this personal relationship to collective death that Greiner believes kept Vonnegut from writing about Dresden for twenty-three years, though there are oblique references to it in his earlier works. Moreover, in *Slaughterhouse-Five* (1969), when he finally does try to use the material as the basis for a work of fiction, he finds it impossible to confront it directly, escaping instead into science fiction. Greiner concludes that he still feels too guilty and too emotionally involved in the event to present it effectively. Greiner also thinks that the "So it goes" phrase communicates the futility the author feels in trying to communicate the meaning of any single death in the midst of the collective death of a community of people.[12]

In the introduction to the novel Vonnegut says that on his postwar journey to Germany he was reading Theodore Roethke's *The Waking* with its sense of destiny and compulsion. The poem suggests the coming to awareness of life's meaning and the existential view that existence logically "precedes" essence, that we must experience what there is to experience before we can define life for ourselves. He also refers to Erika Ostrovsky's *Celine and His Vision*, commenting on Louis-Ferdinand Céline's desire to freeze time and his feeling that "truth is death." Looking through the Gideon Bible, Vonnegut sees a parallel between himself and Lot's wife, turned to a pillar of salt for looking back at Sodom and Gomorrah, the victim of her all-too-human curiosity and pity. Dresden proves too much and Vonnegut is unable to deal with the experience. He "freezes" before the awful truth of man's mindless destructiveness, and his hero Billy Pilgrim distances himself in time and space from the event into the realm of fantasy and Tralfamadore.

Some readers of *Slaughterhouse-Five* saw it as a plea for pacifism. Not so. Although he subtitled the book "The Children's Crusade," suggesting that those who participated were innocents sent to the slaughter for a holy cause mismanaged by those in power, he never preaches a return to Eden or finds in his Tralfamadorian universe any Utopia of the spirit. Tralfamadorian omniscience does not create a better world, merely a more complete awareness of the essential Mannichean nature of this one. Though World War II involved him in the Dresden firebombing, many years later in an interview with Robert Scholes, Vonnegut said that World War II was a good war. At the same time, however, he agreed with Scholes that the worst thing Hitler did was to make war creditable again.[13] Vonnegut's view of man and history is pretty much that of the detached historian, who sees man's actions as the manifestation of historical forces that are much larger and deeper than he is generally aware of.

From the first, Billy Pilgrim appears to be fatalistic under pressure. He helps the other POWs clean up Dresden after the firebombing and then is released to go home. Just as fatalistically he becomes a successful optometrist and has a "bearable" marriage before his wealthy wife dies. Unfortunately, however, Billy cannot forget the horrors of Dresden.

At intervals he finds himself transported in time to another planet. There he learns the Tralfamadorian concept of time, which reinforces his fatalism and helps him cope with his guilt. After learning from the omniscient Tralfamadorians that the universe will be blown up by a Tralfamadorian test pilot and finding that no one can prevent it, Billy is advised that the Earthlings might do what the Tralfamadorian do and "ignore the awful times, and concentrate on the good ones."[14] Tralfamadorians see all the time at once, focusing on whatever part of it they choose.

The Tralfamadorian view of time helps Billy overcome his compulsion to redeem history. If the end result is preordained, if each moment is an entity unto itself, and if each can be given its own value according to the individual's way of looking at things, then one can, by limiting one's expectations and one's sense of responsibility, cope with life on a day-to-day basis. The similarity of this view to the "one day at a time" principle for recovering alcoholics is not accidental. Billy is recovering from battle trauma. As James Lundquist has pointed out, the Tralfamadorian "hallucination" is Billy's way of coping.[15] Nevertheless, one does not learn from adversity by refusing to acknowledge it. Adherence to such a view puts the individual at the mercy of the forces he cannot help but fear. The result is a split reaction between the intellect that tries to substitute a partial reality for a whole one and the emotional self that is traumatized by the part that is being repressed.[16]

Like Hemingway's shocked war veterans, Jake Barnes in *The Sun Also Rises*, and Frederic Henry in *A Farewell to Arms*, thought is too painful for the hero, and the perceptions must be carefully selected for him to avoid thought. But, whereas, the Hemingway heroes focus on an immediate present and try to build their lives anew on the maximization of pleasurable responses to the activities of sex, sport, travel, and conviviality, Vonnegut's Billy Pilgrim lives a split life, shifting between the conventional activities of family and career, memories of Dresden, and the fantasies of Tralfamadore. In their own ways, though, both Hemingway's heroes and Vonnegut's Billy Pilgrim are seeking to fulfill the prescription Billy finds in Montana Wildhack's locket: "God grant me the serenity to accept the things I cannot change, courage to change the things I can, and wisdom always to tell the difference."

The narrator of *Slaughterhouse-Five* tells us that Billy cannot change the past, present, or future, which makes the prescription meaningless, but one of those falsehoods, or "foma," that we live by. In an interview with *Playboy Magazine* in 1973 Vonnegut said "There is [in our culture] that implication that if you just have a little more fight, the problem can always be solved. This is so untrue that it makes me want to cry—or laugh."[17] For Billy, as for Eliot Rosewater, history has been a tragedy, and like Eliot he feels encumbered with a dreadful guilt for the failures of American idealism. Eliot Rosewater feels morally responsible for the failure of the American dream of its capitalist individualism to promote the welfare of the less able citizens. Billy Pilgrim cannot rid himself of the shock of Dresden, of the American willingness to unleash mass destruction on a hapless and unthreatening community of human beings. The dream has failed economically, politically, and morally because the dream extols the virtues of individual self-realization and power at the expense of self-limitation and social responsibility, because the focus is on the individual free self and not on the establishment of community and cooperation.

For Billy, as for Céline, "time is death." Time is history, and history surely appears to be creating a technologically produced, exponentially raised power of destruction for humankind. Billy knows that his own death at the hands of a misguided avenger will occur on the thirty-first anniversary of the firebombing of

Dresden. He is also told by the Tralfamadorians that the death of the universe will occur at an inescapable moment in the future.

For Hemingway, Camus, and other Existentialists death is final for the human being. The life factor in the Existential algebra, where life finally equals zero, can be increased, however, by living life intensely. And though death comes to all life forms, Hemingway, at least, took comfort in the passage from Ecclesiastes that assures us that the Earth abideth forever. He also suggests, quite mystically, that love in full intensity, as in the love of Jordan and Maria in *For Whom the Bell Tolls*, and in the oneness the fisherman feels for his magnificent prey in *The Old Man and the Sea*, are moments "forever." There is then in Hemingway a truth at the base of things that may be touched intermittently in moments of intense revelation that make us aware of our unity with the elemental forces of life and the universe and that assure us of a kind of immortality. We are, after all, ineluctably a part of the Scheme of Things, whatever that Scheme may amount to, however the mixture of opposing forces may be carrying it out or developing it.

Vonnegut only goes so far as to say that "the Universe is an implied Something with man on earth at the center of it."[18] Vonnegut's all-knowing Tralfamadorians have little interest in Christ. They are more interested in Darwin and in the idea that corpses are improvements. Billy knows that he will become a kind of prophet of an advanced society, only to be killed by an assassin sent to avenge the death of Roland Weary, the soldier who tried to kick him into motion in fleeing the Germans during World War II. Billy's prophecies will have no lasting effect; the universe will be destroyed all the same. Billy speaks of himself in his prophetic role as "Wild Bob," a reference to a dying colonel who spouted patriotic balderdash in the midst of death until his own.

Lest we think Billy's simple-minded prophecies of a better life have merit, Vonnegut presents a series of ironic scenes near the close of the novel. There is a passage from Harry Truman's Hiroshima speech, with a scene in which Billy Pilgrim, the optometrist, is examining the eyes of a Mongoloid, a passage in which an old man is in agony because he is so blown up with gas, and a scene in which Billy's reformed, juvenile delinquent son stands proudly before him in a Green Beret uniform.[19] Others follow.

Billy has trifocal vision. His view of present, past, and future is not united. He is haunted by the shock of war, jarred into alternate dreams of hope and nightmares of despair for the future of man, and at the same time leads what is to outward appearances a successful middle-class life as an optometrist and family man. Billy Pilgrim comes to adopt the Tralfamadorian saying about the mixture of good and evil in life, "So it goes," but he cannot successfully blot out all the negative events and concentrate only on the good ones. He has no feeling that the intensity of a moment gives him linkage with an acceptable timeless truth. He cannot abandon his idealism nor can he believe in it, which accounts for his disunited perspective. As Eliot Rosewater says, Dostoevsky is not enough.[20] The

American hero, the "pilgrim" of the New World is looking for something more than an endless cycle of crime and punishment, control and rebellion, a chance to go beyond individualism and vengeance to social cooperation and tolerance, from rejection to acceptance. In the end he clings to the hope that there are some undefined things that he can change.

The free will question is once again at the heart of Vonnegut's next novel, *Breakfast of Champions* (1973), which he says was made out of materials left over after "decanting" the prose of *Slaughterhouse-Five*.[21] In this book Dwayne Hoover, a car dealer, becomes paranoid due to "bad chemicals," and after speed-reading Kilgore Trout's book *Now it Can Be Told*, in which the Creator of the Universe has created every being as a robot except one, a YOU, which Hoover takes to be himself, Hoover goes beserk. Exercising what he supposes to be his own free will, he wreaks vengeance on those he thinks have wronged him, including his mistress and a black who thinks of him as his savior because of his automobile advertising. Hoover injures eleven people before he is apprehended by a policeman. The free-willist is relieved by the arrest and thanks God for the policeman's presence. The message is the same as that of Dostoyevski's Grand Inquisitor: most humans cannot stand "freedom" for very long. Even the most oppressive authority offers some degree of security that the unrestrained, uninhibited individual, at the mercy of his own impulses and compulsions and the resulting chaos, will be impelled to seek.

Old Trout with his venous legs and sense of failure is ever the optimist, however. In a men's room he reads a question, "What is the purpose of life?" and he wishes he could write, "To be/ the eyes/ the ears/ and conscience/ of the Creator of the Universe/ you fool." His conscientious sense of human responsibility gets him nowhere, though, and because of his miserable life his author lets him know that he is setting him free at the end of this novel. This "freedom" for Trout may not be any better than it is for Dwayne Hoover; it is an exile to emptiness, for characters like people have their being in the interplay of conflicting forces of personality and place. Moreover, one could argue, that by setting his character free the author is simply severing the lifeline. The character is now lost at sea or missing in action, his life not free but gone except, very literally, in the pages of memory.

Trout has his say, though, before his release (and he does reappear in *Jailbird*). He tells us that life is dangerous but not necessarily serious. When he gets his feet covered with plastic from a polluted river, he does not get upset. He tells a truck driver that God is no conservationist, so to be one would be sacrilegious. Trout is known to speak with his fingers crossed, like his author, just for the hell of it, and this may be such a case. But God is a God of absurdity, and to be sacrilegious is to be for human caring and responsibility against the absurdity of an uncaring universe. Trout is more likely thumbing his nose at You Know Who just as Bokonon did in *Cat's Cradle*.

American misbehavior is largely due to "bad chemicals," we are told. These "chemicals" may be drugs, alcohol, or the "breakfast of champions." They are, in fact, all the "gunk" that we swallow to function in our society. They are the slogans of free enterprise and rugged individualism that make Hoover's perception of Trout's appeal to free will so injurious. They are whatever we thoughtlessly ingest that limit and distort our awareness of human need and capability. *Breakfast of Champions* carries the same message as William Burroughs's *Naked Lunch*, though the style is totally different.

The final word in *Breakfast of Champions* belongs to Rabo Karabekian, the minimalist painter who defends his art as representative of the "awareness of every animal—the 'I am' to which all messages are sent . . . all that is alive in any of us . . . unwavering and pure. . . ."[22] We are then told that ecstasy blooms on his barbaric face. He has discovered what five-year-olds already sense in their innocence, which we lose as we grow older. To keep our awareness and to awaken again the sense of wonder that brings in the world afresh, we need to recognize and control the "bad chemicals."

A sense of the "I am" without relation to the needs of others, however, leads to egomania and destructive lawlessness as seen in Dwayne Hoover's rampage. Rabo's look of ecstasy is both a look of truth and madness. The child is a savage, and the "bad chemicals" of capitalism, encouraging selfishness and greed, will cost him not only his self-awareness, but will fail to civilize him as well. In fact, to be civilized, a person must have an enlarged awareness of self, a self in context with the rest of society, a self whose needs are met through mutual dependence with others and with obligations willingly incurred and fulfilled. Our competitive society with its emphasis on individualism looks upon cooperation as a temporary expedient, limited to the task to be performed; obligations incurred are often unrecognized or easily cut short when they no longer seem expedient. Such a society will, as de Tocqueville noted a century ago, become highly litigious, looking to the law and its enforcement for equity among its citizens and as a means of defining the limits of social cohesion. Ecstasy or not, Rabo's face remains barbaric, and Dwayne Hoover welcomes the policeman's appearance.

For Vonnegut, the mid-seventies were a time for taking stock after the youth revolt of the sixties and the acclaim that it brought his novels. He gathered his ideas on writing, life, and society together in *Wampeters, Foma, and Granfalloons* (1974), emphasizing man's need for brotherhood and for a sense of universal justice. He iterates his belief that the universe must be man-centered if it is to have meaning for man at all. There is a confessional element too to this collection of statements, previously given addresses, and *Playboy* interviews. He admits to his basic sentimentality and to a feeling of guilt about his tolerance to all points of view. He seems to wish that he could express righteous indignation about the state of affairs, but the Tralfamadorian perspective makes that emotion unsupportable for very long.

By the time he came to write *Slapstick* (1976), the confessional impulse was upon him with a vengeance. The first chapter is autobiographical, and the whole book reads like the nervous breakdown of a mind too long at odds with itself. He attempts to fictionalize his own schizoidal feelings in the characters of a pair of monster twins, whose forced separation destroys their brilliance.

Vonnegut says he never learned to love. His mother became crazy when he was young, and he missed the affection of a nurturing parent. The monster twins are isolated from the parents until their fifteenth year, presumed mentally retarded and catered to by the servants. When they do display their actual intelligence, they make their parents feel guilty. When the twins are separated to encourage their individual growth, they lose their natural complementarity and their fused brilliance. Eliza, the intuitive one, never learns to read or write. Wilbur goes on to medical school. Vonnegut's own feelings of self-alienation are shown in this split. One has the feeling reading *Slapstick* that the author wishes he could share the sense of wonder and fanciful dreams of his youthful readers, but the Wilbur side of his own educated self prevails, and, with a guilty sense of betrayal, he follows out the flower child romanticism of the sixties to its irresponsible and foolish end.

As a student of anthropology under Dr. Robert Redfield at the University of Chicago, Vonnegut became an admirer of Redfield's "folk societies," primitive societies in which all humans are treated as persons, not things, and in which the environment itself is personalized by their religion and intimacy with nature. Vonnegut sees man as biochemically induced to seek folk-society association and to be frustrated without it.[23] In *Slapstick* Wilbur tries to overcome his personal sense of isolation and the loneliness of a science-dominated, bureaucratized society by giving the same middle name to individuals with like interest, thus creating "families" of hundreds of assorted individuals. He runs for President and is elected, using the slogan "Lonesome No More." Wilbur is displaced from power by the "families" of common interest who are soon at war with one another just as the states of the world have been for centuries. The same inevitable tendency, noted first in *Player Piano*, for authoritarianism to give way to anarchy and to become authoritarian again is shown in *Slapstick*. Cooperation turns into competition; peaceful association becomes an alliance for war. Man turns out to be less dangerous when lonesome and isolated than when joined in a common cause. In the end Wilbur's granddaughter arrives, a fairy princess named Melody, clutching a Dresden candlestick like the Grail, but she is a pregnant fairy princess and the Grail is soon broken. The Daffodil "family," of which Wilbur is a part, breaks up.

The author speaks through his character Wilbur with the disillusionment of the Johnson years: "Aside from battles, the history of nations seemed to consist of nothing but powerless old poops like myself, heavily medicated and vaguely beloved in the long ago, coming to kiss the boots of psychopaths."[24] Vonnegut felt out of touch with the young and equally ineffectual in dealing with the older generations. *Slapstick* is the nadir of Vonnegut's disillusionment with history and with himself.

Love is so fraught with uncontrollable, conflicting desires and divided loyalties in its application and so amorphous and misleading in the abstract that Vonnegut will not plump for it as a desirable virtue, though he seems to regret not having known a close, affectionate love relationship in his early life. He says that in the final analysis love is unimportant. What is needed is common decency.[25] In the introduction to *Jailbird* (1979), his retrospective novel, published three years after *Slapstick*, he quotes a fan of his, a high school student named John Figler, who says he encapsulated the meaning of Vonnegut's novels into the statement, "Love may fail, but courtesy will prevail."[26]

In *Jailbird* (1979), the "old poop" of *Slapstick* has blended a Tralfamadorian fatalism with a kind tolerance and amused wonder at the absurd twists and turns of events, has filtered out the dregs, and has presented his readers with vintage Vonnegut.

This novel too opens with a preliminary, confessional introduction which grounds the themes of the novel in personal biography. Vonnegut tells us that he once wrote a story using his father and mother as characters. The father was nine years old, all eyes and hands, easily bullied, and the mother was an ignorant sixteen. Sensations meant more to his father than ideas, and the mother lapsed into madness and death, he says, because she declined to go on living without being one of the richest women in town. The parents were immature, unintellectual, and unaware of the social problems of their time. In reaction to their social indifference, at an early age he settled on his own heroes, John Dillinger, who was regarded as something of a Robin Hoood, and Powers Hapgood, the labor organizer, who became such, he said, because of The Sermon on the Mount.[27] In the novel Walter Starbuck will return to prison for believing in The Sermon on the Mount.[28]

Starbuck, who bears the name of Melville's Calvinist first mate of the ill-fated *Pequod* in *Moby Dick*, finds the ways of the universe hard to fathom, feels the pull of divided loyalties, suffers the curse of conscience, and is overpowered by self-centered men bent on their own destruction. This Starbuck of Vonnegut's book is no New England Puritan, however. A descendent of East European immigrants, his rise and fall are due very much to his American opportunism. As a boy he plays chess with millionaire Alexander McCone, who promises to send him to Harvard, and does. He is led on by visions of attaching his displaced self to the class of people who lead the country. In government he serves both Roosevelt and Nixon.

At Harvard he follows the fashionable intellectualism of the time, becoming a Communist sympathizer, and, then, after the Hitler-Stalin Pact of 1939 changing his views to a cautious belief in capitalist democracy. In his later years he admits that he remains an idealist, and a fool.[29]

In the 1950s, when he testifies against Leland Clews, a Yale graduate who has taken away his girl, he falls out of favor with his Ivy League classmates. To make up for his earlier act and because he is depressed by his wife's death, he refuses in the 1970s to tell Watergate investigators who secreted a trunk full of a million dollars in his White House basement office. For this refusal to testify he is sent to Finletter Federal Prison.

When Starbuck is released from prison, he meets his old sweetheart, Mary O'Looney, who poses as a half-starved old woman who collects junk in her shopping bags. Actually, she is a very rich widow, Mrs. Graham, who controls the assets of the all-powerful corporate conglomerate RAMJAC. Upon her death he buries her with her will that would give all her holdings "to the American people." Starbuck thinks the government too heartless to run the business enterprises for the benefit of the people. "The economy," he says, "is a thoughtless weather system—and nothing more."[30] After working as a vice-president for RAMJAC, his burial of the will is discovered, and he is once again on his way to jail.

Mary O'Looney Graham was one of Starbuck's young loves; the other was the self-centered, rich Sarah Wyatt. Employees of Sarah's father died of radium poisoning, as did Mary O'Looney's mother. Mary O'Looney is the impractical social idealist. Sarah, on the other hand, reminds one of Jasmine Washington in F. Scott Fitzgerald's story, "A Diamond as Big as the Ritz," horrible in her selfish innocence. They are both dangerous to the common welfare, but it is evident that Vonnegut's heart is with the beneficient shopping-bag lady, Mary O'Looney, a female counterpart of Eliot Rosewater without Eliot's guilt.

As in *Player Piano* the technological elite in government and industry run the nation. RAMJAC and the "gut-wrenching" roar of planes on the air force base next to Starbuck's prison are continual reminders of their dominance. As *Player Piano* also showed, there is no way of erasing the elite. Any attempt to destroy its organizations simply results in new accretions of power. Starbuck says that his own division of RAMJAC is "being snapped up by I.G. Farben, a West German concern."[31] (This is probably also Vonnegut's backhanded way of praising Pynchon's *Gravity's Rainbow*, which did snap up his own "division" of the subject of technological dehumanization.) The Arabs have also bought MacDonald's hamburgers.

The passage of time has affected certain values and beliefs, however, both Starbuck's own and those of society. Upon his release from prison Starbuck finds that the restaurant next to the Arapahoe Hotel where he took Sarah in 1931 is now a place where homosexual films are shown. The room clerk, a crummy-looking Phi Beta Kappa, takes him to the "bridal suite," a repainted room where a prostitute was murdered. The waiter in the refurbished restaurant wears a *légion d'honneur* ribbon like the one Starbuck wore to prison but gave away when honor became meaningless in its relativity. Love and honor are degraded. The lower classes and their anarchic lawlessness appear to be in ascendancy. Later, when he says at a party that people do not give a damn anymore, they laugh at him, as though he is a fool to expect it.[32]

Starbuck has emerged from prison after Watergate hoping to make sense of history. Throughout the hotel scenes we are given flashbacks to the jailbird's earlier life, to the depression, to the war, and then back to the present. Dates are spelled out with great ceremony, as though they had special meaning, landmark dates in Starbuck's history if no one else's. The effect is of a man trying to reestablish himself, to find some continuity and belonging with his society, a society that seems, like himself, to have found traditional concepts of loyalty, love, and honor insupportable, but unlike himself, to have gone past even caring to preserve a sense of human decency.[33]

Jailbird is the world-weary author's testimony of faith. In spite of the way the world goes, we can learn to be kind, as Rosewater said. If in the long run we are all doomed, in the short run we are committed to life, and that commitment entails its obligations. We simply do have to give a damn. Against the egomania of Ahab and Nixon, Melville and Vonnegut have opposed the moral concerns of the two Starbucks.

In his mixture of American opportunism and moral idealism, Walter Starbuck captures the essence of the American character as defined in such works as Van Wyck Brooks's *America's Coming of Age* (1915), John Steinbeck's *The Winter of Our Discontent* (1961), and Arthur Miller's *After the Fall* (1964). In *America's Coming of Age* Brooks sees the development of American culture as divided between the opportunism and emphasis on material improvement of Benjamin Franklin and the quest for Godliness of Jonathan Edwards. Americans, he said, had one eye on God and one on the till. Steinbeck's Ethan Allen Hawley lost his social position through his own honesty and lack of business acumen. He finally strikes back by seizing business opportunities at the expense of moral obligation and the trust of friendship. In his family there was an ancestor who scuttled a ship for insurance and there was also a severely moral aunt. In Miller's play, Quentin, who possesses the confessional consciousness of the play, tells us of his infatuation with a neurotic, beautiful, famous actress and his use of her needs to compensate for his own sense of failure, of his idealistic innocence in the thirties, of the trial of conscience undergone by those who testified at the McCarthy hearings in the fifties, and of the loss of innocence and the need for self-forgiveness.

Starbuck is successful through his associations with wealthy and prominent people. He fails because he is caught is conflicts of loyalty, morally weakened by disappointments in love, and unable to conceal or express the truth effectively as the changing political situations ambiguously require. Where the clocks of history beat a time that is out of joint with man's heartfelt needs, his only recourse is to keep his own time, to listen to his own *Mannleinlaufen*, as Starbuck's clock is called, and perhaps to keep the faith, if he can, of an eight-year-old child who has heard The Sermon on the Mount.[34]

In his most recent work, *Deadeye Dick* (1982), Vonnegut gives us a farewell to the midwest and a kind of epilogue to the failure of American idealism. The book ends with the statement that we are still in the Dark Ages.

The union of an undemonstrative, wealthy woman and a handsome make-believe artist (materialism and idealism) has produced Felix, a once-successful NBC executive, who becomes a much-divorced drug addict, and the narrator, Deadeye Dick, who at the age of twelve accidentally killed a pregnant woman with his father's Springfield. Vonnegut is once again modeling on his own parents and creating a Rosewater-like guilt complex for his protagonist.

The father's foolish "heroism" in publicizing his parental guilt for the death leaves the child with his own legacy of guilt he must work out by serving his parents unto death. He is dutiful and emotionally stunted. He is a neuter whose response to the destruction of Midland City by a neutron bomb is that it looks about the same to him. Everyone of any consequence had left the place, and he had been ostracized by those who were left. Following his father's advice he had become a pharmacist, only to find that drugs were to cause his brother's failure and Dwayne Hoover's wife's suicide (along with Dwayne's desertion). His mother dies of uranium poisoning, the result of money-saving ingenuity on the part of the house contractors and government misfeasance.

In Midland City the arts are defeated, things are created and saved, and life is annhilated. Those immigrants, like the Maritimo brothers, who came and prospered also destroyed and died in their ignorance. John Fortune, heroically holding to the dream of selfless love and perfect peace, left Midland City for Shangri-La, only to discover personal misery and death in Katmandu. The sole survivor in Midland City is the ghost of a barnstorming aviator who crashed and is now, too late, looking all over town for his parachute. This is the legacy of rugged individualism and the end of the myth of the American hero.

Throughout Vonnegut's novels there are parallels to the works of the French absurdist Albert Camus. Camus's Meursalt in *The Stranger* (1942) is the unfeeling product of a bleak, sterile, mechanical civilization. Caught in a position where he believes he must defend himself, he kills an Arab, and the court convicts him of murder. It is his lack of feeling that convicts him, as it is Howard Campbell's in Vonnegut's *Mother Night*. He is "used up," *l'homme épuisé*, a man who is unable to love, who feels he shares with the universe a brotherly indifference, and who is finally stifled by the unimaginative, mechanical "justice" of the state.

In *The Plague* (1947) Dr. Rieux serves the town of Oran during an outbreak of the bubonic plague in the early 1940s. He cannot reconcile the misery he sees with the idea of an all-powerful and beneficient God as the priest tries to. Nor can he say Rambert, the journalist, is wrong to try to escape to his love, but for Rieux there is only one action and that is to do his job, to try to heal the sick. Rambert goes to work for Rieux and does not isolate himself as Vonnegut's Campbell did, in a "nation of two." Rieux says that, in the final analysis, what motivates himself is "common decency."[35] Starbuck makes an equivalent statement in *Jailbird*.

Rieux works hard against the plague, and his medical colleagues develop a serum to fight it, but nothing really seems to stop it. It simply loses its virulence and subsides. Rieux's labors are not unlike those of Sisyphus, who serves as

Camus's archetypal hero of the absurd. Camus says of Sisyphus, "His scorn of the gods, his hatred of death, and his passion for life won him that unspeakable penalty in which the whole being is exerted toward accomplishing nothing."[36] Sisyphus's triumph is in knowing that "his rock is his thing"[37] just as it is Rieux's "thing" to try to heal the sick, and Rosewater's "thing" to try to be kind, and Starbuck's to try to minimize the pain his actions must necessarily cause others; both of the latter serve their society in their own distracted ways. Camus tells us that the struggle uphil, even though it must be repeated time and again, "is enough to fill a man's heart. One must imagine Sisyphus happy."[38] It affirms life; the rock is in his own hands; he is doing what he is meant to do. Vonnegut's view of man's fate is indeed very similar.

Nevertheless, though Vonnegut has much in common with the French Absurdist's point of view, his work is very American in the subjects that it treats. It is the hallowed myth of American rugged individualism that he attacks most rigorously in *Player Piano* and *God Bless You, Mr. Rosewater*. Rugged individualism and laissez-faire capitalism have eventually created the mechanized corporate state in *Player Piano*, and now the emphasis is on conformity to the point of rebellion. In *God Bless You, Mr. Rosewater* the immorality of early capitalism creates in turn a guilty liberalism that is in its own way just as corrupting of the virtures of self-reliance, prideful work, and a belief in self-realization as the most bureaucratic, technological corporation. Taken together the two books indicate very strongly that the American dream was not ever possible for a large segment of the population. So long as human endowments differ markedly in intellect, temperament, and environmental conditioning, and so long as the more able control the allocation of resources, there will be invidious disparities in earned wealth, personal freedom and opportunity, and realized human potential. That unbridled capitalism should ever have been thought of as the way to realize the American dream for all Americans is in itself absurd.

That Americans should also think of themselves as making the world safe for peace and brotherhood by waging war and building up an increasingly destructive technological capability is also absurd. The politics of Wilson, Roosevelt, and Truman are in many ways as schizophrenic as the politics of San Lorenzo in *Cat's Cradle*. The governor declares the need for armed strength while his people endure pressing social problems. He declares a messiah of peace and brotherhood an enemy of the state, but at the same time he worships him. The disappointed messiah confirms the governor's doubts by leading his people to death.

Soft liberals and hard conservatives both come out badly in these books. American politics has seemed to oscillate between the two extremes, often during the same presidency. Innocents go to the slaughter in *Slaughterhouse-Five* in what the author nevertheless calls a just war, and it is not the flower children of *Slapstick* who will ensure our safety.

The crisis of conscience that propels Paul Proteus to revolt in Vonnegut's first novel is similar to the sense of mission Malachi Constant has in the *Sirens of Titan*, and that Eliot Rosewater and Billy Pilgrim have in succeeding works. The moral revolt is always the result of a too-sudden awareness of evil and an acute attack of guilt. The resulting reformist mission is visionary, unthought-out, and doomed to failure. In *Mother Night* and *Jailbird* entrapment in the conflicting loyalties of politics bring on the crisis of conscience, but the visionary alternative is not really available to the characters who are personally threatened with ostracism and imprisonment. In *Mother Night* the crisis leaves the man exhausted and without resources. In *Jailbird* the character has learned to cope with these vicissitudes and still retain a belief in his own feelings of conscience. If the moral certainties are not so certain after all, he has nevertheless an awareness of self that goes beyond the primal scream and includes ties, however poorly understood, to the rest of his society. Howard Campbell, looking for heroism and trying to match a Platonic conception of himself, as Fitzgerald's Gatsby did, loses his identity and sinks out of sight. Walter Starbuck, seeking identity with the ruling classes, finds identity in the awareness of common human needs and limitations. The tender conscience of untried idealism, the messianic complex of a 200-year-old country of successful revolutionaries, and the collapse of individualism and self-reliance in a world of relative and changing social and political values seem a peculiarly American plot. The plot's events arise out of the absurd differences between perception and fact, the perception being structured by eighteenth- and nineteenth-century conservative and liberal ideals that only partially prove out in their attempted realization.

Chapter 4
The Ironist

Vonnegut's early stories, most of which are science fiction, and collected in *Welcome to the Monkey House* (1950), were written to make money. Various trends in society are blown large and shown in comic-horror dimensions, but the treatment is so simplistic and puerile, the targets so outrageously broad, that the stories fall flat long before they end. So, in "Harrison Bergeron" the pressure for equality has caused the government to handicap its men of genius with weights and electric shocks, and in "Welcome to the Monkey House" women have been so conditioned to preserve their youth and hate sex that they have to be shocked into sexual awareness through rape and be conditioned to use the birth control pill in place of an antisex pill that cuts off all affect.

A sentimental respect for the innocent's vision of a world easily set right with a change of heart is even more evident in some of these stories than it is in the novels, where the grim truth always undercuts the romantic vision. In "The Barnehouse Effect," in which Professor Barnehouse turns his psychodynamism not only against enemy armaments but against those of his own country, there is a triumph of conscience for the preternaturally powerful. In "EPICAC" the noble computer falls in love and dies a sacrificial death. The stories show at an early stage Vonnegut's concern that man's inventiveness may have outstripped his ability to control it to good ends. The only cures offered are outside the system, the arrival of the Great Man who will set things right, in the case of Barnehouse, and an infusion of humane feeling into the machines which help to master-plan our economy, our defense, and our lives, in the case of EPICAC. To rely on miraculous changes in the heart of man for a corrective to man's natural tendencies to exert a selfish power through his inventions suggests the author's doubt that such changes can be effected by normal, believable means. The core of Vonnegut's black humor is here, but the grimness of the situation is not so heavily drawn as it is in his novels, so these stories seem merely light and sentimental.

Regarding Vonnegut's use of science fiction in the novels, James Lundquist says that his mode offers Vonnegut great freedom in demonstrating his vision of the human predicament and that it also makes that situation less frightening than if he had grounded it in a purely factual reality.[39] Willis E. McNelly says that Vonnegut uses science fiction to help us distance ourselves from the otherwise too emotionally involving problems he wishes to discuss.[40] Perhaps it should be pointed out that Vonnegut need not have used science fiction to achieve "distance." All broad comedy creates a "distance" from reality. Science fiction is another convenient way of simplifying a general human predicament through caricature and exaggerated effect. It may be more or less frightening than reality; for instance, consider H.G. Wells's *The War of the Worlds* and the effect on the radio audience when Orson Wells dramatized it in the 1930s. Because Vonnegut treats science fiction in a comic way, with his caricatures of Tralfamadorians looking like plumber's helpers, for example, his characters' reflections on the state of human affairs seem less than dire.

In *Slaughterhouse-Five* Rosewater says that science fiction writers are helping man to "reinvent" his world. In *God Bless You, Mr. Rosewater* Rosewater also lauds the science fiction writers for dealing with the big questions, though he also says that they write poorly. Vonnegut uses science fiction in *The Sirens of Titan* and *Slaughterhouse-Five* to open up the question of a purpose in the universe, the problem of man's morality in an amoral universe, and the adjunctive question of free will. The extraterrestial domain in his novels shows what present scientific and social Earth trends may become, offers a detached perspective on Earth's condition as we look at it from the viewpoint of extraterrestrial beings, and suggests alternate modes of perception that might be opposed to our normal human view of ourselves. Vonnegut makes it very clear that space and technological invention are not escapes from Earth's problems. They magnify those problems rather than reducing them. *Ice-nine* and exotic rocket fuels only bring us closer to universal destruction. Space exploration only brings us closer to the war of the worlds.

In his novels, as his own view of the world's situation becomes less apocalyptic and more resigned, the science fiction element diminishes until in *Jailbird* we are limited to a single reference to Kilgore Trout's fiction. *Player Piano*, of course, develops present trends into an imaginary future society much in the manner of Aldous Huxley's *Brave New World*, but the work that follows it, *Mother Night*, shows us clearly that Vonnegut's chief concern is with the course of human history and with man as the moral center of his own universe, not in his love of gadgetry (unlike the work of a science fiction writer like Ray Bradbury, who often seems enthralled with invention for its own sake). *The Sirens of Titan* is the most imaginative of the works, and it is most purely a science fiction piece. In *Cat's Cradle*, *ice-nine* is a kind of Dr. Heidegger's experiment gone awry. In *Slaughterhouse-Five* space exploration is metaphorically Billy Pilgrim's "spacing out" under the trauma of the Dresden experience. Science fiction there becomes a means of presenting schizophrenia. In *God Bless You, Mr. Rosewater* and works after *Slaughterhouse-Five*, the mode gives way almost entirely to earth-bound satire and farce, and the fantasy world of the characters is pretty much limited in reference to their actual lives.

Therefore, although Vonnegut was early tabbed as a science fiction writer, it would be wrong to categorize him as such. Science fiction is merely one of his devices or modes, and he certainly is a much more penetrating writer than those we usually classify under that rubric.

Vonnegut's use of various fantastic plots and the mixture of prose, verse, cartoons, epigrams, and mottoes that we find in such works as *Slaughterhouse-Five* and *Breakfast of Champions*, to name two where all the elements exist, have caused some critics to call him a pop artist in the Andy Warhol vein.[41] Certainly the collage technique of pop art is similar, and both Warhol and Vonnegut try through the use of the technique to make the viewer concentrate on the nature of his response to the symbols of joy and power of media advertising and propaganda. We are asked to look at these mottoes, symbols, and the actions of cartoon caricatures in isolation, scene by scene, as though the videotape of a segment of a TV commercial were being stopped for a moment at strategic places for us to ponder the real effect of the image just seen. Vonnegut enhances the effect by juxtaposing contradictory elements that expose the foolishness of our expectations. In *Slaughterhouse-Five*, for example, Billy, doped up on morphine and having just urinated, feels ready for a religious experience. He sees a mystical sign in the dark, and it reads (written in the text as a poster): "Please Leave this Latrine as Tidy as You Found it!"[42]

Pop artists and Vonnegut share a concern for the way our minds are manipulated by the powers of advertising and politics through the mass media. *Breakfast of Champions*, which is the most like pop art in its construction, is chiefly concerned with this theme. The popularity of Marshall McLuhan's *Understanding Media* (1964) and his prophecy that our electronic culture would make books obsolete may have served to strengthen Vonnegut's concern in the late sixties, the period in which materials for *Breakfast of Champions* were being brought together.

That book is written with the author speaking directly to the reader and to his character and includes a number of crude drawings of basic items of our civilization. It is as though Vonnegut were addressing the book to some future space explorer who might find the ruins of our world and wonder what to make of them. By presenting the work in this way to the contemporary reader, he is forcing him to look at his world as though for the first time, in a very primitive way. This style is designed to circumvent our usual patterns of response, to make us see what things and processes factually are and what they do, not what advertising and politics tell us they do.

Throughout Vonnegut's books the simplified characters and the use of brief scenes in a collage of different types of expression, coupled in most of the works with the author's intimate storyteller pose, create a sense of easily understood communication to the reader. The ideas presented are not simple, but presented in this fashion and without much reflection on the reader's part, their complexities may easily be disposed of or overlooked entirely. It is partly for this reason that Leslie Fiedler characterized Vonnegut's work as a bridge between high art and popular culture.[43] James Mellard sees these aspects of Vonnegut's tenchique as both his strength and his failing.[44] Both critics believe that these elements help to account for his appeal to the young high school and college readers in the sixties and seventies.

Benjamin DeMott, among others, has also noted the pernicious appeal of Vonnegut's sentimentality to the young.[45] These Mirandas of our "brave new world" saw Eliot Rosewater as a kind of saint, Billy Pilgrim as a real force for love and peace, and, if they are still reading Vonnegut and have not matured, they are no doubt in love with Mary O'Looney in *Jailbird*. To the young who want to believe that all that is needed is a change of heart to make all things right, the bitter pill of man's confused mortality is easily sugarcoated with the treacle of wonder and innocence, and black humor dissolves in images of Rosewater playing Prospero and Billy Pilgrim on a distant planet with ever-loving Montana Wildhack.

At the risk of being identified as an intellectual lightweight, Vonnegut enlists the techniques of science fiction and pop art in the service of serious satire. Vonnegut says that he writes to reduce his own anxieties and to work out his own paranoia about what the powerful people in the world are doing to the rest of us.[46] He sees the artist as a kind of canary in the coal mine, more sensitive than others to the evils of our civilization. Art is a means of schooling young minds against war and social injustice, and it helps man to build useful illusions or "foma" to live by, giving him a sense of usefulness and importance that the overall function of the universe does not indicate.[47]

Vonnegut has taken writers to task for the senseless violence of their tales because he believes that the writer does much to create "acceptable" patterns of behavior in his readers.[48] One might say, though, that in Vonnegut's absurd world there is also a lot of "senseless" violence—for instance, *ice-nine*, the bombings of Dresden and San Lorenzo, and Dwayne Hoover running amuck—but it is all used to make the point that even in an absurd universe we can learn to be kind, as Eliot Rosewater says. Vonnegut's appeal to the younger generation is not the pretentious appeal of a social revolutionist like John Dos Passos, who said that the writer's function is to "set the mind of tomorrow's generation" and in so doing be "the architect of history."[49] It is, rather, an appeal to look at the world afresh, to trust one's own senses and one's own reason and not to let the power brokers and their propagandists break a person down into something less than human. When the canary in the coal mine shows signs of suffocation and collapse, it is a sign that the mines down which we go to find the black jewels of success are unsafe. Another way must be searched for. There is no guarantee that there is another way, but we can at least recognize the dangers and the foolishness of persisting on a path to immediate destruction.

Vonnegut's critic Conrad Festa sees Vonnegut as a Menippean satirist, one whose work has a serious center of moral outrage at man's tendencies for self-deception.[50] Like Menippus, the third century B.C. Grecian satirist, Vonnegut's work attacks contemporary institutions, mixes prose and verse, and often slips into authorial digression. It is a more informal and genial kind of satire than the Juvenalian or Swiftian modes.

One reason for the apparent mildness of Vonnegut's satire is his tendency, as Leslie Fielder says, "to temper irony with sentimentality and to dissolve both in wonder."[51] But the key reason, and the reason why he tempers irony with sentimentality, is that for one who sees the universe deterministically, as Vonnegut does, there is no blame. There are no villains, and, hence, there is no one to be held accountable. Vonnegut dramatized his own deterministic limitations in *Happy Birthday, Wanda June* (1971), the best of his unsuccessful plays. In the introduction Vonnegut says that reading Edgar Lee Masters's *Spoon River Anthology* when he was twelve years old awakened in him the realization that all characters had to be what they were. Speaking of the play, he says, "The intolerable balancing of characters and arguments reflected my true feelings: I felt and still feel that everybody is right, no matter what he says." He goes on to cite *The Sirens of Titan* as already reflecting this point of view.[52] In the play itself Harold Ryan is a caricature of the safari-loving Ernest Hemingway, who believes the world has gone soft and scoffs at the present-day heroism as shooting the village idiot in a pressure cooker to the moon.[53] His antagonist Dr. Woodley say that Harold Ryan is an anachronism and that the new hero is the healer not the destroyer, that love and understanding will make the world beautiful. He calls Harold comical, and wounded in his pride, Harold threatens to kill him. Woodley finally believes Harold and pleads for his life. Harold focuses his hostility on himself then and threatens to commit suicide but is not successful. Woodley and Ryan both appear to have a partial hold on the truth, but through their blind exaggerations and their inability to prove a point, they both appear as comic failures.

Human destructiveness worries Vonnegut. He would like to be able to come out strongly against the views of Harold Ryan and Senator Lister Rosewater, but he knows that pride and self-reliance are virtues just as much as are self-sacrifice, sympathy, and cooperation, and that the two sets of virtues are often opposed to one another. He does think that his own generation went too far in its tolerance of a destructive individualism but cannot bring himself to condemn the rugged individualism of the past entirely.

There is a strong tendency for Vonnegut's characters to balance each other out and for them to lead lives equally composed of family and things, fantasy and heroism, and futuristic vision and painful memories of past calamities (best seen in Billy Pilgrim but also present in Rosewater, Proteus, Constant, Campbell, and Starbuck). In *The Breakfast of Champions* Vonnegut says that once he discovered how misled people were by the "stories" they were told about the nature of American life he "resolved to shun storytelling. I would write about life. Every person would be as important as any other. All facts would also be given equal weightiness. Nothing would be left out. Let others bring order to chaos. I would bring chaos to order, instead, which I think I have done."[54] Now, while it is true that Vonnegut never really drops the storyteller pose, and all the facts are not presented (how could they be?), the intent to present a balanced perspective on the results of the American dream is clear. That those results are indeed very mixed is also clear. The order of the dream dissolves into a changing equilibrium of opposed psychological, social, and political forces.

Vonnegut's satire then is a balanced attack on human pretensions. It finds no heroes and no villains, just human beings in the grips of illusions, which when treated as absolutes and acted upon consistently will lead man to ruin. Just how belief works out in practice is the source of Vonnegut's irony. Paul Proteus becomes a convert to revolution only to find that revolution will again create the industrial state. Malachi Constant sees himself as the elect of God, and when his elelction is confirmed, he finds that the God he serves destroys brotherhood, drives men to murder, and is in many ways wholly unpredictable. Eliot Rosewater tries to fulfill the demand for Christian love only to drive his wife to revolt and himself insane, while he leaves little lasting impact on those he has aided. "So it goes."

The basic irony in these plots lies in the irreconcilable opposition to fate by human beings who demand an absolute prescription for their lives in a relative universe, who want permanence and unity in a world of change and fragmentation, and who want harmony in a world of dialectical conflict.

The ironic impetus to his writing has always been there. The early science fiction stories show the same tendencies. In the 1950s Vonnegut sought out story subjects the way a cartoonist would.[55] This method may also account for the brevity of the scenes in his novels. Each scene is drawn to make its point, set off by extra space and often some sort of colophon, and then the next scene in the sequence is presented. John Leverence counts 28 separate anecdotes filling 140 pages in *Cat's Cradle* alone.[56]

These "anecdotes" are what Vonnegut calls his "jokes."[57] They are terse descriptions of ironic situations, sometimes capped with ironic statements. Each one is designed to bring the central character and the reader along to the point where he can confront the inescapable absurdity of life and laugh at it. As Robert Scholes puts it, "What man must learn is neither scorn nor resignation, say the Black Humorists, but how to take a joke."[58]

These "jokes" are often used to make a moral point; hence they also have the quality of the fable. Aesop's "The Fox and the Grapes" might serve as a model. In the introduction to *Jailbird* Vonnegut tells of his father wanting a piece of wood from an old house that was being torn apart, how he was given the wood by the wreckers, how he pulled out all the nails he could see and then had the wood ripped into boards at the mill. The saw hit a hidden nail and he had to pay for a new blade and belt. Vonnegut says his father's moral tales were like this one, "neatly packaged and self-contained as an egg."[59] Vonnegut Junior tries for the same effect, and like his father's tale, his own anecdotes and scenes parody the vanity and greed of human beings, also often parodying their pride of knowledge, including the author's own.

William Veeder says that Vonnegut lacks subtlety and that he is insufficiently detached from his character in *Mother Night*.[60] He also says that Vonnegut's irony is self-indulgent and didactic. By contrast, he says that Vladimir Nabokov is subtle and detached from the character of Humbert Humbert in *Lolita* and we come to know the pervert as part of ourselves in a way that the reader can never attain with Howard Campbell.[61] Certainly Vonnegut is neither so subtle nor so complex as Nabokov. As to whether the reader is apt to identify more with Humbert Humbert or not, one might say that is a matter of taste. Vonnegut's characters are vehicles for his ideas more than characters in the sense of being imaginable human beings. Their predicaments are nonetheless intriguing. The appeal is principally to our recognition of the caricature as representative of a type of human being faced with a very basic and troubling ethical dilemma. The author's intimacy with the reader is a way of asking him to consider the problem together with another troubled and engaging human being. The didacticism that Veeder objects to is that of a teacher who stands with his pupil at a blackboard and solicits his involvement in solving an equation.

David Goldsmith has run through the characters in Vonnegut's work and noted that he "rarely describes a character is much detail, being content for the most part to present one vivid physical image." This is even true of the major characters. Our first acquaintance with Billy Pilgrim, for example, is with an ill-clothed soldier, six feet three inches tall, with an upper torso like a box of kitchen matches, gawky and red-faced like a flamingo. Goldsmith says that these images are striking but that they call attention to themselves and do not really help to develop the character.[62] One thinks of Charles Dickens's Uriah Heep, Wemmick, Lady Haversham, Peggoty, and the like, and he has to admit that the satirist can do more to make the caricature fit the character it is supposed to represent.

Because of the cartoonist's method of apprehending and presenting his material, Vonnegut is also very terse in describing his scenes. Unlike Camus in *The Plague*, who is very careful to build the details of his scenes and uses the repetitive acts of rats and people dying horrible deaths to impress us with the horror of the situation, Vonnegut gives us only a brief description of the firebombing of Dresden, a few grisly particulars, and then the escape into his Tralfamadorian hallucination in Billy Pilgrim's consciousness. Even the science fiction scenes are tersely described, enough to give us the *idea* that Vonnegut wants to present but not enough for us to feel the emotional reality of the experience.

The author's approach to experiences is basically an analytical one. James Lundquist, among others, thinks that Vonnegut shows "the increasing gap between the horrors of life in the twentieth century and our imaginative ability to comprehend their full actuality.["]63 Whether Vonnegut suffers like many of his readers from an unwillingness to deal in detail with the traumatic, or whether he simply prefers to make his point intellectually, the result is that we are less moved than intrigued by his novels.

Like his fellow Absurdist Thomas Pynchon, Vonnegut uses names to designate character types. Paul Proteus is a protean man, whose allegiances change over a period of time. Eliot Rosewater's name suggests Christian preoccupations. The first name suggests the Puritan preacher Eliot, preaching to the Indians, not so unlike Rosewater as he preaches the gospel of love to his social outcasts, and, of course, the call to reaffirm traditional faith that T.S. Eliot gives us in his twentieth-century poetry. The last name consists of symbols of love and baptism, but it is also the name of a bath oil, suggesting that the effect may be more cosmetic than intrinsic. Billy Pilgrim is involved in a quest for religious meaning as were the biblically named Malachi and Jonah before him, though, as Stanley Schatt has pointed out, there is not much comparison to be made in any allegorical sense with Christian in *Pilgrim's Progress*. In fact, it would be wrong to try to force an interpretation of Vonnegut's work in that direction. His similies, symbols, and names are not extended into any formal pattern.[64] In his next to last novel, *Jailbird*, Arpad Leen is a kind of anagram for kneel-and-pray, Leen making Mrs. Graham (Mary O'Looney) his idol of corporate worship because of her order to "acquire." Perhaps the jumbled spelling suggests that Arpad is kneeling to the right God but for the wrong reasons, since her intent is to destroy the corporate power of private business, not to enhance it. Walter Starbuck, of course, shares the name of Melville's man of conscience, opposed to the egomaniacal Ahab in *Moby Dick*. Starbuck is also one who bucks the system and can make a buck as well. The guiding star of conscience, never, unfortunately, in the same place in the mixed-up heavens of our uncertain time, completes the name and essential character of the protagonist. Other names, such as Mary O'Looney, also show the ambivalence of the characters, the illusory quality of their beliefs and their misguided behavior.

After *Player Piano* and *Mother Night*, in 1963 *Cat's Cradle* began the series of works written in a fragmented back-and-forth time sequence. Some of these are without chapter divisions, but all treat time as a composite of intermingling states of perception. Present awareness moves readily into memory and into fantasy. There is also a continual intermingling of history, authorial autobiography, character action and thought, and authorial comment on the character. This fluid form permits the author to indulge himself in anecdotes and digressions and to let his characters follow a flexible line of development.

The rationale for such "organic" writing is based on the belief that the imagination provides insights that the straightforward presentation of the truth inhibits. The imagination may, in fact, be our salvation when the so-called truths have become insensible. Vonnegut has also said, "If a person with a demonstrably ordinary mind, like mine, will devote himself to giving birth to a work of the imagination, that work will in turn tempt and tease that ordinary mind into cleverness."[65] Vonnegut is, however, not a spieler in the fashion that John Barth is; nor does he project such extended flights of fancy onto the screen of an historical period as Pynchon does. His use of the imagination is always guarded, limited by his cartoonist's desire to get the point across in a simplified and brief way. The terminal point has been formulated ahead of time, and the characters are destined to arrive at it after a number of stops along the way to pick up passengers and to look briefly at the view. We take no roads to get lost for a time, simply to see where they come out, as we do with Pynchon and Barth or, for that matter, in the longer picaresque novels of Saul Bellow.

The style of the remorseful Absurdist, Kurt Vonnegut, is essentially analytic and ironic. In his novels human beings are merely a part of an indifferent scheme of things, who refuse to believe that fact. Recognizing how defeating such knowledge must be to human aspirations, Vonnegut faces the truth regretfully and supports the necessity of "foma," or illusions, for man to live with a modicum of happiness in his life. His irony is undercut with sentiment and the belief that even if man cannot expect more than an indifferent or paradoxical answer, he can at least make sure his side of the dubious bargain with fate is conducted in good faith.[66] He can learn to see the world in all its discreteness, its multiplicity, its chaos, and he can learn to substitute better illusions for those which are dangerous to his well-being. In this last respect the supreme irony in Vonnegut's work is the same as that of Mark Twain's *A Mysterious Stranger*.[67] Human beings need to fool themselves in order to live. We look for a "supreme fiction," in Wallace Stevens's term, to help us cope with a contradictory, essentially frustrating and destroying, reality.

Chapter 5
In Quest of the Self

In Barth's seminal story "Lost in the Funhouse," thirteen-year-old Ambrose finds that in the funhouse mirror-room he cannot see himself go on forever in the mirror reflections because his head always gets in the way. Even with a periscope the image of the eye would always cover whatever he wanted to see; Ambrose looking can only see Ambrose looking. The subject becomes the object, and Ambrose becomes the prototype of Barth's self-conscious heroes in a solipsist universe.

Ambrose cannot go through the funhouse enjoying it as his brother Peter and his girl friend Magda do. They unthinkingly accept the curious mirror versions of themselves and the occasional pratfalls as a stimulus to their own sexual gratification. The funhouse, as Ambrose notes, is for lovers, lovers of the immediate play of sensations, not for those who have a great sense of self-importance or who are thoughtful and questioning. Much as he would like to be an unthinking participant in the explorations of sexuality, Ambrose is too much a thirteen-year-old J. Alfred Prufrock for this to occur. His "head" is always in the way. Even earlier in the toolshed, where Magda apparently played with his genitals, he had to *tell* himself that he was feeling passion; his desires are immediately shunted into self-conscious contemplation. To one who feels so inept in fleshly pursuits, it is awful to think that the sole purpose of the funhouse world is its continuation through those very same activities. The dummy Fat May's infectious mechanical laughter proclaims the unthinkable truth.

Ambrose feels trapped and his father gives him no advice. His one glimpse of a man who is possibly the funhouse operator shows him an old man half-asleep, obviously uncaring and not in control. Ambrose finds it deplorable that people could get lost or hurt engaging in their amusements.

In the funhouse Ambrose loses his name coin, suggesting a loss of idenity. He is left behind by Peter and Magda (whose biblical names suggest enduring faith and sexuality), and feels that he was wrong to think of himself as a person. He has discovered that his own sense of self depends upon his perception of how he is regarded by others, and he feels suicidal.

In the mirror-maze he finds a name coin with his name on it. He thinks that it was discarded by someone else, no doubt the former self he has left behind, for here in the mirrors he finds what he could not find in the mirror room—"the endless replication of his image." He is literally lost in reflection on a multiplicity of selves as he tells endless versions to himself of the adventures he is having. He has found self-extension possible through imagination and art just as the author does through his fiction. He will replace the funhouse operator by designing fictional funhouses of his own that are complicated but controlled. Life for Barth, as for the author of "Prufrock," is to be controlled through the artistic imagination.

His art will have limitations, however. The imagination is not unbounded. The replicated selves in funhouse mirrors are a regression to infinity, growing smaller and smaller until blurred and imperceptible. Moreover, they are essentially copies of the still intrinsically unknown original. Self-knowledge will reach a point of diminishing returns and self-projection a point of vaguer and more abstract human dimension.

Epistemologically, the "I" is always ultimately regressive in its contemplation of self, for the contemplating "I," once mentally conceived, shifts from subject to object. We, in fact, suppose a subject, a knower, which is really a set of relationships among percepts immediate and recalled. There is no final "I" to be known unless it be that very sense of life that Arthur Schopenhauer, the German philosopher, called the Will and Bergson the *élan vital*, a primal drive to consciousness that Barth so agonizingly celebrates in the sperm's journey toward the egg in "Night Sea Journey."[1]

In the essayistic piece, "Echo," Barth suggests in the myth concerning Echo, Tiresias, and Narcissus, that we are all beguiled like Narcissus by a "reflection," or like Tiresias by false voices, or unable to go beyond the words of others as is Echo. "Our story's finished before it starts."[2] Watching a self-projected, wish-fulfilling image of ourselves, unable to sort out true from false, and locked into a language and patterns of thought not of our own making, we are largely prohibited from original achievement. Barth speaks here not only of the general human condition, but also of the plight of the artist, as one finds it in his more famous essay "The Literature of Exhaustion."

In "Anonymiad" the nameless minstrel is abandoned on a deserted island with several jugs of wine, memories of his women, and little hope of rescue. He slaughters goats and writes on their hides his own versions of Greek myths, stuffs them in the empty jugs, and sets them afloat on the sea. An admitted solipsist, he is painfully aware of the limits of his knowledge, but in the act of sending out his "messages," whether they are read by others or not, he thinks there is an act of self-affirmation that makes the effort worthwhile.

The relationship between sex and art, between procreation and creativity, is strong in all of Barth's works. In this story the minstrel "humps the jug," filling it with his semen, before filling it further with his written "messages." The blind force for self-extension that he describes in "Night Sea Journey," frustrated sexually, as it is in "Lost in the Funhouse" and "Anonymiad," is sublimated into art.

Barth's characters are exceedingly self-conscious, preoccupied with feelings of failure and in revolt against their limited possibilities and the human condition in general. They also tend to be emotional cripples, converting the simplest human responses to impossible formulas for self-conceived proper action. Mind and body are sharply split and antagonistic to one another in most of his characters.

Todd Andrews, the first of Barth's novelistic antiheroes, suffers from heart disease, a sign of his inability to feel spontaneous affection. Like Camus's Meursalt in *The Stranger* (1942), his motivation to kill arises out of a psychoneruotic fear of self-annihilation, a final, desperate assertion of self that would not only be self-destructive, but would lash out and destroy, once and for all, those barely comprehended personalities that seem to diminish him in his own eyes.

In *The Floating Opera* (1956; revised 1967—all references here are to the revised edition), Todd is enormously self-centered, proud, and identifies with no one except longingly to a dead father he never really knew. He mistakes ideas and ideals for practical action, and has little spontaneous feeling. He has, he says, known, *categorically,* mirth, fear, frustration, surprise, and despair prior to his attempt at suicide. After failing in his attempt, he learns to accept his limitation. His attempt at self-destruction is precipitated by his rejection by the one woman who has fully accepted him as a lover, Jane Mack. Her initial acceptance was not spontaneous, however. It was prompted by her husband's desire to experiment with a triangle love relationship to prove his own liberalism. When she withdraws her favors, Todd must have a sense of having been manipulated and humiliated, though he does not recognize these feelings as the core of his despair.

Todd learned mirth early, when in his first act of intercourse at seventeen he saw himself and his partner in a bedroom mirror. Todd's laughter, to judge by his generally repressed condition, may not only reflect the incongruity of thinking man making the beast with two backs but may also be defensive as well. If sex really were laughable, then the sexual performance would not be very significant. But in spite of his attempts to make himself and his audience believe that sexual success is easy if one puts his mind to it, and that sexual rejection is merely the playing out of the last cards in a game of love, he cannot feel that this is so. His emotional reaction is deep-seated despair and dreadful hostility toward the floating opera world that ignores his hunger for fulfillment.

Todd, like the speaker in "Night Sea Journey," contemplates suicide. Like Albert Camus, the creator of Meursalt, Todd asserts that suicide is the first question for a philosopher to face, for he believes nothing in life has intrinsic value.[3] He feels keenly the failure of his father to serve as a life model when the latter committed suicide. Moreover, he wants to "discover the extent of my father's contribution to our imperfect communication."[4] The loss of the father theme, symbolic of a loss of religious faith and of a belief in traditional patriarchal authority, was prevalent in the literature of the forties and fifties in such works as Hemingway's *For Whom the Bell Tolls*, Bellow's *Seize the Day*, and Bernard Malamud's *The Assistant*. Like the central characters in those authors' books, Todd feels impelled to discover his own first principles, and like Bellow's Tommy Wilhelm he nearly loses his life in despair.

Feeling rejected by his father's suicide, Todd is mistrustful of all apparent affection. Suspicious of Harrison Mack's professed satisfaction at how his wife expresses her love for the two of them, Todd tests him by telling him that he, Todd, is acting as lawyer for a black woman and accepting her favors as payment. Later, on the proposed day of his suicide, he suggests that Mack have his wife make old Captain Osborne happy before he dies. Mack is suitably upset that Todd thinks of Jane Mack as a prostitute, but Todd's skepticism never rests. During the war he killed a German soldier out of mistrust, after the man fell into his foxhole and they had embraced as war-weary soldiers feeling a common brotherhood. After that event, he discovers that he has endocarditis and is given a medical discharge. He is relieved to hear that any moment might be his last and pays for his hotel room by the day, "reminding myself that, for me at least, goals and objectives are without value," and as the day closes with his writing in his *Inquiry,* he is also reminded "that the fact is irrelevant." His work on the *Inquiry* (which, after all, is Barth's), makes him feel "a little bit outside of time and heartbeats" because "processes persisted in long enough tend to become ends in themselves."[5] For the emotionally stunted skeptic and for the writer unsure of his audience the means of going on is to substitite process for purpose as did the abandoned minstrel in "Anonymiad." In the case of Todd Andrews, unable as he is to build his own boat and forced to accept the world of Captain Adam's *Floating Opera* showboat, the answer is what Barth calls elsewhere "Scriptotherapy," a substitution of words for action and the world of the mind for the world of fleshly pursuits.

Todd tests the ethical protestations of Harrison Mack. He also tests the Shakespearian actor who vows that he will finish his speech delivered before the unruly crowd on the showboat by joining the crowd as they throw pennies at him. Finally, he tests his own courage in his resolution to end a life that is purposeless by preparing to blow up the showboat with himself and 699 others on it, including the Macks. When his plot fails, he feels neutralized. He has asserted himself to the extreme, but his fate is in the control of forces larger than himself.

Todd has spent much of his life trying to elude those forces by adopting various masks and by playing various roles. He finally admits that "all the major mind changes in my life have been the result not of deliberate, creative thinking on my part, but rather of pure accidents...which I afterward rationalized into new roles."[6] Indeed, Todd is the first of Barth's great roleplayers. As such he is well aware that the impressions others give are often the impressions of roleplaying as well. The masks he has adopted, he says, were "to hide my heart from my mind and my mind from my heart," to perpetuate a near-fatal division of reason from emotion, of mind from body. In the process he has played the roles of rake, saint, and cynic to cover up his mistrust of, and longing for, human ethics and sexuality.[7] Critic Charles R. Harris interprets this insecurity as a schizophrenic response to the world that necessitates the playing of any number of roles so as to keep one from being held and manipulated by others.[8]

Aware as he is of the human proclivity to perform and to accept performance as truth, he is not relieved or disappointed when his attendance at the minstrel show on the *Floating Opera* ends not with a bang but with the mimicking antics of Burley Joe, whose name is close to being a cognate for Burlingame, the arch-roleplayer in *The Sot-Weed Factor*. If life is an illusion, it is not so easily dispelled. Todd's *hubris* in taking it upon himself to end a purposeless existence, not only for himself but for the rest of his world as well, is countered by the self-perpetuating force of illusion, or in Oriental terms *maya,* which, though it may be purposeless, is still all that we have to know and work with in our sensory existence.

When old Mr. Haecker ceremoniously overdoses himself, Todd thinks he is also playing a role to give his death meaning. Todd concludes, after failing in his own suicide attempt and after watching Haecker's playacting, *"There's no final reason for living (or for suicide)."* [9] (Barth's italics.) The question of suicide becomes meaningless. Life *is* and so is death. Neither one is justified. We are simply part of the process. Ethically, he considers "whether, in the absence of absolutes, values less than absolute mightn't be regarded as in no way inferior and even lived by."[10] After preparing for sixteen years to write his account of his life, Todd tells the reader, "Everything, I'm, afraid is significant, and nothing is finally important."[11] In short, Todd has come to accept truth as relative, inter-subjective, endlessly interlocking, and without a definite cause or purpose.

In his story, "Menelaiad" (in *Lost in the Funhouse)*, Barth makes two points that underscore Todd's predicament. First of all, Menelaus learns that love requires a willful, blind tolerance, for when he asks Helen about Paris, her Trojan abductor, she says that Paris's Helen was a cloudy form made by Zeus to fool Paris. Menelaus chooses to believe her story, playing the willing fool, for love of the woman who chose him of all her possilbe Greek suitors. Todd on the other hand, lets his skepticism curse whatever demonstration of affection he might otherwise enjoy. Also, in the "Menelaiad," Menelaus discovers, after his encounters with Proteus, Eidothea, and Helen and after listening to the involved tale of Peisistratus, that he cannot really know the truth about Helen since her identity is so endlessly refracted in the eyes of others. Not only can he not know her without contradiction, but what is seen in others' eyes is what she becomes. One's identity then is dependent upon the way he is perceived by others. The roleplaying that both Mr. Haecker and Todd indulge in is motivated by a need to establish a personaly acceptable identity through the reflection of self in the responses of an audience. Audiences are fickle, though, and what they see of the self in the roles of the Floating Opera world will lead to multiple interpretations. One should then not take the effects of one's roleplaying too seriously, as Todd has done.

In his next novel, *The End of the Road* (1958; revised 1967; all references here are to the revised edition), Barth deliberately set out to counter what David Morrell has called Todd Andrews's "brave ethical subjectivism."[12] Barth says that he was reading Robert Musil's *The Man Without Qualities* with much appreciation in these early years of his writing, and Musil's book may well have had some influence on the structure and philosophy of the work. Frederick G. Peters has compared Musil's central character, Ulrich, to Dostoevski's underground man; both are so intellectually aware of the ramifications of alternatives that they cannot make a decision. Barth's Jacob Horner suffers from the same disability, which Barth calls "Cosmopsis."[13]

In *The Man Without Qualities* Ulrich, who denies the value of rational categories, is opposed by Walter Arnheim, who is systematic, makes choices easily, is seemingly well-balanced and gracious, but is involved in his business mergers and expansion in supporting a war. The character of Walter Arnheim is based on the life of the engineer-industrialist-philosopher Walter Rathenau, whom Musil met aroung 1913.[14] Rathenau was to be influential in the kaiser's government and, later, in the Weimar Republic as a democratic socialist. Rathenau also appears under his own name in Thomas Pynchon's *Gravity's Rainbow* (1973), as a spirit who has realized that his dream of merging the national spirit and technology to bring about a utopian state was mistaken. Musil found in Rathenau a prominent figure who represents the capacity of the intellect to mask irrational desires, allowing the personality to present itself as controlled, logical, and self-secure while at base it is insecure, trembling with frustration, and ready to sacrifice all to its own dream of rational order and balance. In Barth's novel Joe Morgan is the irrational rationalist who opposes the vacillating Jacob Horner.

In *The Floating Opera* Todd Andrews masked his fears and frustrations with his rationalizations and with a compulsive attention to detail. After killing the German soldier, he became convinced of his own animality and thought that that event might account for his own later belief in systematic procedures. Even while contemplating his suicide and the blowing up of hundreds of other people in the process, Todd carefully attended to the details of his law practice, in spite of his cynical awareness that the law is a system that can be manipulated according to whatever desires one has for it. He had already demonstrated this cynical knowledge in his handling of the Mack family lawsuit and in manipulating the suit between Morton and Butler so that Morton ended up suing his own son. In the *End of the Road* Todd's tendency to rationalize his choices to maintain a sense of command over his destiny is given to Joe Morgan while Jake Horner absorbs Todd's skepticism and wary aceptance of man's essential selfishness.

Like Todd Andrews, Jake Horner narrates his own story. He says of himself that his forte is "articulation." ". . .to turn experience into speech—that is to classify, to categorize, to conceptualize, to grammarize, to syntactify it—is always a betrayal of experience, a falsification of it; but only so betrayed can it be dealt with at all, and only in so dealing with it did I ever feel a man, alive and kicking,"[15] Horner tells us. Horner, then, is another author-surrogate, like Ambrose Mensch, who while recognizing that the operations of speech generalize and contort the actual effects of experience, also recognizes that his ability to shape experience to his own designs is a necessary self-assertion for the contemplative man.

Moreover, Horner, as a character in a work of fiction, needs all the self-assertion possible. Paralyzed with indecision, he has been undergoing the black doctor's "Mythotherapy." The doctor has ordered him to play roles and to make arbitrary choices to get him in motion again. The doctor is not interested in the causes of his paralysis. He cites Wittgenstein's dictum, "The world is everything that is the case," and adds, "what the case is is not a matter of logic."[16] When a role no longer seems suitable, the doctor says, Horner should switch to a new one. The doctor is telling Horner to substitute experience for purpose, action for contemplation.

If he must read, the doctor advises that he read Sartre, presumable for Sartre's emphasis on the need to find a suitable code of existence for oneself and for Sartre's emphasis on the value of human choice. After taking a job as a grammar teacher at Wicomico State College as an act of engagement with the world, Horner makes a comment about Sartre's axiom "existence precedes essence": "Existence not only precedes essence: in the case of human beings it rather defies essence. As soon as one knows a person well enough to hold contradictory opinions about him, Mythotherapy goes out the window."[17] In other words, if a person has trouble defining another person's character, he will have trouble defining his own role in relation to the other person, so roleplaying, or Mythotherapy, becomes anxious and confused. Mythotherapy might work if one could be disengaged, but the whole point of the therapy is to bring one into fruitful relation with his fellows, with the opposite sex, and with the world in general.

The roleplayer may also seem confusing to others. Joe's wife, Rennie Morgan, says Jake puts on and takes off masks and cancels himself out. She says he has no center, that he is nothing. On the other hand, her husband Joe, she thinks, has a coherent personality. Joe is not so coherent, however. Jake and Rennie watch him through a window upon his return from a boy scout meeting. In this scene Joe makes faces and dances before a mirror, finishing his not-so-private roleplaying with a final return to a primitive self in masturbation.

Roleplaying, then, is a normal human activity, and the ego is always a mask. The doctor tells Horner that if he sometimes feels that his mask is "insincere," it is only "because one of your masks is incompatible with another."[18] Be that as it may, Jake feels insincere and guilty in his relationship with Rennie Morgan and cannot, or will not, find a role to carry himself away from those feelings.

Jake's problem is similar to that of the Absurdist James Purdy's Malcolm. In *Malcolm* (1959), a book that apparently owes much to Barth's *The End of the Road,* Malcolm, like Jake, is found sitting on a bench unable to exert his will sufficiently to move. He is befriended by a black undertaker who gives him a list of addresses to call upon in order to get him in motion, but after a number of encounters with strange people who take only a polite interest in him, Malcolm is rejected by a man whom he takes for his long-lost father and dies. Mythotherapy and address therapy both lead to the end of the road, which is the final nonanswer to the "why" of life, unanswerable for Malcolm, for Jake, and for Joe just as it was unanswerable for Todd Andrews and for Ambrose Mensch. None of them can, in the final analysis, accept a random experience as a value in itself. All seek conviction, a center of self, a self of fixed principles that work toward human happiness.

Joe Morgan, the athletic history teacher, claims that he does not believe in absolutes. He believes, he says, that subjective, relative values for the immediate situation are the only values we can really have.

According to Morgan, the chief difference between French Existentialism and American Pragmatism is not just personal but cultural energy. "—where the hell else but in America could you have a cheerful nihilism, for God's sake?"[19] Joe is indeed an energetic American Pragmatist, more in the nature of John Dewey than William James. Like Dewey he believes that whatever a person does is what he "wants" to do at that moment, that he always chooses the alternative he thinks or feels best at the time. Choices may be very limited, however, because both physical and psychological circumstances tightly circumscribe possible actions. In order to insure the best long-term choices, the person must be educated to understand these circumstances and to see the possibilities as fully as possible.

Joe's wife is his student. He plays Pygmalian to her Galatea. She is to carry out Joe's Pragmatism in action. Pragmatism, as one of its tenets, demands that whatever is thought to be true be tested. An idea is only true if it proves itself in practice. Joe carries out this side of the philosophy with a vengeance, first, by testing Rennie's supposed self-sufficiency with Jake's maleness and skepticism, second, by socking his wife on the jaw for apologizing for having sex with Jake and not having the strength of her convictions, since she had to be doing what she wanted to do, and third, by sending Rennie back to Jake to "do it again," again to prove her convictions and to disprove her self-sufficiency.

Morgan is trying to make an absolute out of a relativistic philosophy. He does not allow for the pressure of circumstances at given moments, for the fluctuation of human feelings, and for the reality of remorse. He does not see, ironically enough, that when Rennie apologizes, that she is doing then what she wants to do just as much as she did what she wanted to do when she had intercourse with Jake. When she is sent back to Jake to "do it again," she is doing what she wants to do but only because she thinks that is what Joe wants her to do and his wish is her command. Joe demands reasons for their conduct. Jake can give no reason. He thinks that what will destroy the Morgans is their terrible lack of imagination. The mixture of circumstance, emotion, and desire is just not reducible to a "reason."

In all of Barth's work sex is essentially a power struggle. It is no accident that Ambrose's first introduction to sex was a game called Niggers and Masters, and that Todd Andrews's sexual fears are largely fears of being held in thrall by a woman who has the power to cast him off. In the sexual triangle in *The End of the Road,* when Rennie assumes a lighthearted attitude about the affair with Jake, Jake and Joe become glum; when she is hurt by Jake's sarcasm, he feels cheerful.

When the game becomes serious and Rennie is pregnant, it is Jake who, out of remorse and a determination to set things right, exerts himself most forcefully, seeking out the doctor to give Rennie an abortion. Horner changes from fatalist to hysterical, existential activist, while Joe Morgan slips into cynical despair. Horner's hysteria and the entire ending of the novel from the battle for the gun in Horner's room to Horner's leaving town is melodramatic, the entire triangle being too obviously a case in point in Barth's assault on the weakness of rationality and the evil inherent in negating other people's acts of choice.

Barth's next novel was *The Sot-Weed Factor* (1960; revised 1967; all references here are to the revised edition). In this work Barth claims that he was trying to "make up a plot fancier than *Tom Jones*" and to write a "big book."[20] The character of Barth's Eben Cooke, however, owes less to Fielding's *Tom Jones* than to his *Joseph Andrews.* Like Joseph, Eben prizes his innocence as a virtue, and, also like Joseph, he has a sister (in Eben's case a twin) who is his spiritual counterpart.

Critics have tried to place Barth's novel in various literary pigeonholes. Russell Miller notes that critics have called the book an "historical novel," an "anithistorical novel," a "mock historical novel," a "shallow parody," and a "geniunely serious comedy." Miller sees it as a mock epic, particularly associated with the *Odyssey* in a number of roughly parallel events. As Miller also indicates, critics have found in it parallels to the narratives of Boccaccio, Rabelais, Cervantes, Fielding, Sterne, and Voltaire as well.[21]

Centrally, what all the critics start from is the awareness that they are reading a parodic treatment of history and of man's attempt to make sense of it. Barth has taken Ebeneezer Cooke's poem *The Sot-Weed Factor* and his own knowledge of the history of his native state, Maryland, as his starting point. Philip Diser has matched the poem against the novel and finds that Barth fairly well followed the sequence of events in the poem. All of Barth's character's poetry is attributable to the original Ebeneezer Cooke. "...Barth himself, as narrator of the novel, presents the poem as commentary on Ebeneezer's experiences in the novel to the point at which the poem is written (approximately halfway through the novel), showing how each section written by the character Cooke describes an incident he was involved in since leaving England."[22] The other historical work that serves the author is John Smith's *The Generall Historie of Virginia* (1624). Joseph Weixlmann has made a detailed comparison of the original and Barth's parody of it, amply showing how thoroughly Barth dissected it for his own purposes.[23]

In John Stark's opinion Barth "produces his most clever historical farce in *The Sot-Weed Factor,* by sexualizing history."[24] The most wonderfully outrageous sexualization occurs in Barth's account of John Smith's encounter with Pocahontas. But he also introduces Thomas More and Isaac Newton as two English university homosexuals, who try to initiate Eben's tutor Henry Burlingame into their fraternity. Later, Barth gives Eben a rougher seaman's homosexual initiation aboard a pirate ship. Throughout, Eben is driven on, at once trying to preserve his innocence and to capture the object of his infatuation, the whore Joan Toast. The motivations of philosophers, explorers, and historians are all seated in sexual frustration.

As seen earlier in "Night Sea Journey," sex is a drive to recover a union lost. The sense of self that Barth plays with throughout his works is a sense of separation from the Other. Sexual union is a way of recovering oneness. In *The Sot-Weed Factor* this separation is symbolized for Eben in his separation from his twin sister Anna, and only when be becomes more worldly and gives up his "virtue" is he reunited with her. The way back from separateness lies through healthy sexuality and a respect for the ways of the world.

Eben's separateness is largely a result of Burlingame's tutoring. By the time Eben goes to Cambridge, Burlingame has made learning such a game that Eben cannot take the facts of history seriously; he can always think of alternative possibilities. He also lacks the capacity for disciplined scholarly study. Burlingame has educated the imagination at the expense of respect for facts. Because of his endless consideration of possibilities, Eben suffers from a form of Jake Horner's Cosmopsis. Because he is naive and not predisposed toward any belief, he is easily persuaded, "at least notionally, by any philosophy of the world, even by any strongly held opinion, either poetically conceived or attractively stated. . . ."[25] It is no wonder then that when Joan Toast has left his room angry at Eben's failure to pay her and treat her as the whore she is, he rejoices in now knowing that the event has made his choice of career, to be a "virgin and a poet; less than mortal and more; not a man, but Mankind!"[26]

Eben escapes from the demands of his sexuality into vaporous idealism. The notion of being a poet is high-flown enough to hold him to his calling, and his fear of animal sexuality and general bumbling ineptitude preserve his virginity for several hundred pages. His rhetorical attempts to equate his art with necessary virginity are comic rationalizations.

His tutor Burlingame escapes from the threat of impotence in his own way. Orphaned and born with inadequate genitals, Burlingame learns to use his wits to develop a compensatory potency in a life of action, disguise, and tutorship. Like Todd Andrews he finds that a deliberate inconstancy keeps him from the paralysis of indecision. He becomes Barth's all-time master of masquerade, popping up throughout *The Sot-Weed Factor* in various guises, as pontificating Peter Sayer, as the unsavory Captain Mitchell's son in the swine pens, as Lord Baltimore, Eben's bemused patron, as Coode, Baltimore's antagonist, and as others who aid in the education of the young man of innocent virtue, Eben Cooke.

Burlingame says, "I have no parentage to give me place and aim in Nature's order: very well—I am outside Her, and shall be her lord and spouse."[27] Like Eben, he attempts to make a virtue out of his displacement from the natural order. Like the sperm in "Night Sea Journey," he feels cut off from "Her." He knows there is no way of finding his way back to the womb or into a sense of oneness with the blind processes of nature. He can learn enough to control her for his own benefit, however, or such is his determination when he tells Eben, "One must needs make and seize his soul, and then cleave fast to it, or go babbling in the corner; one must choose his gods and devils on the run, quill his own name on the universe, and declare 'Tis I' and the world stands such-a-way! One must *assert, assert, assert* or go screaming mad. What other course remains?"[28]

Burlingame has three aims: to search out his father, to educate Eben, and to involve himself in the affairs of the world in such a way as to help maintain its balance of political forces by his being first on one side and then on the other. Burlingame says, "... I love no part of the world ... but the entire parti-colored whole, with all her poles and contradictions. Coode and Baltimore alike I am enamored of, what e're the twain might stand for. .... "[29] He goes on to say that he loved not Eben or his sister separately but together, and he also sees the twins as lusting after each other in a desire to become one, a view, incestuous as it is, that Eben cannot accept.

Burlingame's view of life is similar to that expressed in Emerson's "Brahma" and "Each and All." It is one that delights in the dance of life and one's participation in it. At once, he appreciates the variety of form and the way that the forms counterbalance one another to make a whole—*compensation* is Emerson's term. He would be like Whitman in *Song of Myself,* both "in and out of the game," both the active and the contemplative man.

Eben is the young innocent who has come to the New World to try his fortunes. He sees America at first as a kind of New Canaan, but after foolishly losing his patrimony and finding the people of Maryland to be comprised of brigands, whores, pirates, connivers, and deprived and hostile Indians, he discovers his own foolishness and completes his poem on "beshitten Maryland."

After the pirate ship episode he is deeply depressed by the loss of lives aboard the ship due to his monomaniacal love of innocence. He has come to realize that one cannot with impunity command other's lives in the pursuit of a personal ideal, the same lesson Joe Morgan should have learned in *The End of the Road*.

Eben then is the innocent of the New World who finds that Adam's fall pertains on the western side of the Atlantic. Burlingame is the New World's self-made man of many parts—individualist, man of action, and believer in the world's rough justice.

In fact, Burlingame's overall purpose in the plot is to keep the game going. His tutorship is designed to make Eben see that there are no absolutes, that all is flux and flow, and that what we know of ourselves and others is often dependent upon our undependable memories.[30] We are in a state of becoming, with past and future both uncertain, caught in a dialectical process in which we have no choice but to play a part if we are to play at all. And to Henry there is no question: we must *"assert, assert, assert!"*

Burlingame, like Todd Andrews after his suicide failure, has concluded that relative values are sufficient. Unlike Joe Morgan, he does not try to make of his own relative concepts a universal dictate for others, though at times his lecturing may sound so. Eben must make his own mistakes. Rennie Morgan is taught by the authoritarian method, Eben by the Socratic.

Burlingame is the author's contrivance and his set speeches the author's voice. His roleplaying, in the words of Manfred Puetz, "makes him utterly diffuse and somehow nullifies him as an individual."[31] Nevertheless, the mode of the comedy is farce, and the characters in such a mode need only be types and devices.

The humor of the novel is the bawdy humor of burlesque, the incongruity of farcical situations, and the language of double entendre. The cast of the humor is "black,"or at least gray, for, as Max Schultz has partially defined this sort of humor, the focus is "less on the individual than on the world of experiences, less on the agony of struggle to realize self than on the bewildering trackless choices that face the individual."[32]

Complicating the choices is the fact that they are never what they seem to Eben. Appearances are seldom reality. Certainty gives way to possibility, and Eben, the idealist-reformer, can only bumble along wishing it otherwise. Burlingame is, however, a greater radical than Eben, at least in the terms of the grammar teacher Jack Horner. Horner says in *The End of the Road* that

> the greatest radical in any society is the man who sees all the arbitrariness of the rules and social conventions, but who has such a great scorn or disregard for the society he lives in that he embraces the whole wagonload of nonsense with a smile. The greatest rebel is the man who wouldn't change society for anything in the world[33]

Burlingame promotes what he finds to be the dialectical laws of society's and nature's flux and flow and makes himself part of them. He is, in the final analysis, less nature's lord and more her spouse, marrying himself to her ways and asserting himself within her context.

Barth's exact descriptions of sailing and battling the waves off the Maryland shore, his scatalogical humor in the Pocahontas episode and in the Rabelaisian feast that Burlingame the First indulges in to save his party from the wrath of the Indians, his fine coupling of historic events and authentic journal passages and poetry with his own foolery, his ability to write the English of the period with great consistency, the spritely dialogue of Hudibrastics, and his complex plotting with nothing out of place are all remarkable strengths in this long novel. *The Sot-Weed Factor* is a showpiece, showing what the author can do with history, language, and plot. It is, however, episodic and, at times, seems endless. Farcical events collect without advancing the theme. Eben seems an incorrigibly slow student, and his rescues from hanging, drowning, imprisonment, and being burnt at the stake through the timely intervention of Burlingame, in one guise or another, are remimiscent of Scott and Cooper at their worst. Much of the speechifying sounds a good deal like Scott's noblemen's monologues, used here to parody the style but at the same time destroying whatever human feeling we might expect to find in the character. In fact, in the reading the characters soon beome boring devices, and the author's virtuoso tricks with history and language are not sufficient to sustain any but the most dedicated reader's interest all the way through. The complex plotting, while a *tour de force,* seems eminently self-indulgent.[34]

Chapter 6
Myth
and Recapitulation

With *The Sot-Weed Factor* Barth had found in the character of Henry Burlingame a stance that accepted relativity, sought active participation in the conflicting processes of life, and, assumed a responsibility for the well-being of those more innocent. It remained to be seen, however, just how far roleplaying could carry the character toward meaningful achievement beyond the education of the clumsiest of innocents.

Barth took as his next subject the matter of heroism, examined the possibilities of roleplaying using myth and allegory, and once again found the prescriptive idealist guilty of the unpardonable sin, which Hawthorne described as the sin of pride and the selfish use of others to serve one's own grand idealism. Barth had already used myth in "Menelaiad" and "Echo" to point up the limits of human perception. In *Giles Goat-Boy* (1966) he used Lord Raglan's *The Hero,* with its categorical stages of the hero's development, to schedule Giles's adventures, the myth of Oedipus to underscore the theme of Pride and Fate, and a good deal of Biblical symbolism to punctuate Gile's moral growth. Barth also used Joseph Campbell's *The Hero with a Thousand Faces,* which applies the biological theme of ontogeny recapitulating phylogeny (or "Cosmogeny") to the hero, who must repeat the educational growth of his race even as he achieves his own heroic identity.[35]

The setting, a university campus, is based on the layout of the Pennsylvania State University campus where Barth was teaching as he worked on the novel. The novel's campus is politicized, divided into East and West campuses, and, as such, becomes a microcosm of the world power struggle. Into the ferment comes a would-be savior, a self-proclaimed Grand Tutor, out of the goat pens of the School of Agriculture, gimping along like Oedipus to save civilization, equally blind, sure to fail.

Blindness to the self, human vanity, and the ineradicable sin of pride are once again central themes. Watching the mock-*Oedipus Rex,* entitled *Taliped Decanus,* Dr. Sear says that Taliped is his Grand Tutor, "stripped of all innocence! Committed and condemned to knowledge!"[36] George (Giles Goat-Boy) is condemned to this fate, but the knowledge he comes to is not what Sear envisions. For George ends without certitude, knowing only that there are no absolutes, that life is flux and flow and balance and conflict. George learns to accept his goatishness as part of his nature, whereas Sear, though he studies man's animality and experiments with it to his own delight, loathes himself for his depravity. For Sear "self-awareness is bad news" but essential for understanding. George is right that Sear loves his self-loathing too much.[37]

Ironically, it is Sear who clips a mirror on George's stick and tells him that the beginning of wisdom is to know there is always another way of seeing things. When George sights down his stick to the new "token," he sees only the reflection of his own eye.[38] George becomes increasingly aware that no matter how many angles of vision one has, they are all essentially, subjectively, one's own. Sear, on the other hand, never gives up trying to find some certain truth. After being partially blinded by cancer, his search turns inward, and near the end he is asking George for assurance that "a kind of spiritedness" is an absolute good no matter what the person thinks, for the "spirited" Croaker, the giant football player, has permanently blinded him but given him what he takes for a kind of mystical insight. George says he is being sentimental.[39] Sear is a miserable victim of Puritan guilt and the Faustian desire to know. In the "posttape" we are told that Sear castrated himself to be closer to Gynander (the mock-Teresias of *Taliped Decanus*) and bled to death thinking he had achieved a prophet's state.

Blinded by their simplistic political beliefs, both Leonid and Peter Greene, the Bolshevik and the American conservative, have only one eye each. They battle over the novel's sex object, Anastasia, the winner to get the loser's good eye. When Leonid's good eye is accidentally slashed, Peter Greene blinds his own good eye out of remorse. The quest for romantic love blinds as badly as political dogma, and guilt finishes the job.

The man of science is also partially blind. Eierkopf accepts Harold Bray as the Grand Tutor because he *sees* with his eyes and his lenses Bray apparently change and walk on water. Then George drives out Bray with his stick coated with reproductive symbols and adorned with lenses and mirrors, suggesting perhaps that the devil's magic can be undone by the appetite and intellect in forceful union. Bray lets out a stream of fetid green liquid and disappears. Eierkopf has again *seen* enough to convince him that George is the Grand Tutor. Science only knows its observations and they change in time. Eierkopf, though, is better off than Peter Greene, who with his one eye lacks depth perception in both the literal and figurative sense and who, with his aversion to mirrors, will never rightly know himself.[40]

The scientist's perception is also limited by his desires for recognition and transcendence. In Eierkopf's case, his whole several-volume study of the egg was motivated by a WESCAC (West Campus Computer) dictum that Commencement begins *ab ovo* and by his desire to regain the good graces of the university administration after the failure of his eugenic experiments. Max Spielman, George's surrogate father, is also a scientist. It was he who pushed the EAT button and fried the brains of the Ameratasus people during the Second Campus Riot. Eierkopf (by birth of the opposite faction, but an apolitical scientist) set the wavelength, and the Russian Chemintinski focused the signal. After the World War II allegorical episode Max, too proud of his own academic specialty, psycho-proctology, falls out of favor with the administration and faculty, is denied academic retirement, and ends up tending the goat barns. He tells George that the smell which George comes to hate is "the stink of the flunked, the stink of the Moishians, and the stink of the goats" and says he hopes George will learn to love them as the *goyim* love their Tripos.[41] Later, when Max is feeling remorse for having killed the fascistic motorcyclist Hermann, he admits that he was getting back at George's mother, Virginia Hector, daughter of the university president, at the establishment she represents, and at studentdom in general by raising George as a goat. Pride and shame, not the disinterested pursuit of truth, motivate both scientist and scholar.

Max thrives on guilt. He says, "Suffering is graduation," and asks for crucifixion. George rightly notes that Max's suffering and desire for martyrdom are Vanity, "choosing himself to suffer for the failings of others, and believing that his own flunked aspects (overrated in my estimation) could be made good by that suffering."[42] Barth is attacking both Judaism and Christianity for their presumption of cosmic knowledge and for their assertion that they have the formula for salvation.

We are all blind out of ignorance, but the blindness that Barth opposes, as do all good satirists, is the blindness that is self-induced. And yet, because the core of the living being is desire, we are all inducing our own blindness to some degree. Our desires focus our attention, and that focus leaves out parts of the whole necessarily.

The character who most successfully undoes his desiring so as to comprehend eternity is the Oriental holy man, the Living Sakhyan (Sackyawn), who in eliminating desire is eliminating self and concern for all other selves as well. Leonid the Nicolayan (Communist) also wishes to eliminate self, but has a strong desire for perfect community on earth. George says, "Leonid's dilemma was thus not unlike mine, or any right-thinking undergraduate's, and I spoke of it therefore with compassion: the wish to achieve perfect self-suppression, like the yen to graduate, was finally a prideful wish and thus self-defeating; to achieve it, not only the self must be suppressed, but the selfish wish itself."[43]

Man is condemned to selfishness so long as he lives. Trying to keep man in a state of innocence will not undo that part of our nature either, as Max found out when Billy (as George was first called in the goat pens) was first sexually aroused and killed Tommy the goat in rivalry over a desirable female of his species. After Max has killed Hermann, Harold Bray says Max has come to understand *"that the heart is flunked; that what it needs is not instruction but Commencement; not a professor but a Grand Tutor, to graduate it out of hand with no Examinations; otherwise all is lost, for however we may aspire to the state of Graduateship, we may never hope to deserve it."*[44] (Barth's italics.) Max in turn, gives up trying to determine whether it is more vain to take the shaft than not to take it and advises Leonid, ". . . don't worry what's selfish what's not. Assert yourself! Embrace. You got to suppress something, suppress unselfishness."[45] The ponderings of conscience lead to the inanition of Cosmopsis and self-defeat. The answer, again, is to choose a course of action, even arbitrarily, but always to assert the self. George's tutor, Max ends up saying the same thing that Eben's Henry Burlingame did: "Assert!"

Max's view that we are condemned by our innate selfish *desiring* natures to commit sins against our fellows and to suffer endless frustration and remorse is the Hebraic view of man, the tragic view, as Barth says. Barth says it is, in fact, his own.[46] Max sees the world as operating cyclically. George, after first attempting to prove absolute right and wrong and then trying to prove that there is no difference, gives up his attempts to discriminate and then to fuse the differences of earthly existence, couples with Anastasia, and, in completing the biological cycle, knows, for the first time, Spielman's Law of Cyclology, perhaps better than Max knew it himself. There is no way of making the circle go straight, no linear progress toward a simple world of right and wrong or all-accepting peace. We are here to "assert" ourselves, to suffer, and to continue. After union with Anastasia, who may be his sister (a recaptured part of the ego, the loving, earthly half), George's mother brings him the amulet of Freddy (the goat's testicles that George lost when he entered the main gate of the university). His animal potency is restored apparently. But this amulet is also the sign of the scapegoat. George has taken on the role of the Jew, of Max Spielman. Prior to this copulation with Anastasia his shōphār loses its horn tip in symbolic circumcision, a sign that the hero has come of age as well and that this union is one of maturity. He says that now he sheds tears not for himself but for studentdom.[47]

At least from the moment of parturition the human knows separation, discontinuity, and opposition. At the same time, he knows that the objects of his perception are related to each other and to the perceiving self, linked in the act of knowing, relative to one another spatially and functionally in time. Moreover, as the perceiver moves and objects move, the relations change, and what was unified may become separated and vice versa. There is ever an opposition of elements in time and space, yet all are potentially unifiable, and when one tries to make the discrimination too fine, as Eierkopf does in trying to find the exact midpoint between tick and tock on the campus clock, the effort is doomed to failure. There is no exact midpoint, no Infinite Divisor; the mathematical regression goes on to infinity.

George tries to do the same thing in setting impossibly fine distinctions for moral passage or failure. The result is campus chaos. If passage requires that one be nearly perfect in goodness and humility, it also requires that one judge that goodness, and George finds it impossible to determine the exact nature of human motivations, unable to separate pretense from fact in others and even in himself. Rebounding from one opposite to another, he then tries to ignore all oppostition, so that passage is failure and failure is passage. The result, again, is chaos.

When the "egghead,"Eierkopf, falls out of the tower, failing in his pursuit of the Infinite Divisor and unable to answer the question as to which came first the chicken or the egg, he falls like a baby bird from the nest. Eierkopf's analytical intelligence is confounded by time and by the cycles of biology. George tells him to forget the Infinite Divisor and to live by instinct, but Eierkopf is smart enough to know that that role is not possible for one as poorly endowed with genitals as he. Eierkopf is only complete when on the shoulders of the animalistic Croaker.

George too suffers from a mind-body disjunction. Love turns to lust and killing in the goat pens. Later at the saturnalian Spring-Carnival Party in the Power Plant the words of passage are read over the body of the Goat-Boy's deliverer, G. Herrold. G. Herrold goes down the chute into the scorching air below, leaving George clutching the shōphār which G. Herrold had held in death moments before. George accepts the symbol of faith and blows it. The ceremony is completed when George mounts Anastasia on the bier and, in the name of the Founder, the sun, and the Grand Tutor, plunges home. Anastasia, love goddess that she is, shouts that she believes in his Grand Tutordom. After the event, however, George is not so sure, and as his stick gets entangled in the whistle cord, the EAT alarm goes off. Man's appetites are in control, and chaos ensues, much to the amusement of Stoker, Anastasia's husband, at ease on the bier which has just become a "loveseat."[48]

Stoker, the head of the powerhouse, presides over this event because it is one that shows the power of man's passions in control. In contrast, Stoker's half brother Chancellor Rexford, the Aristotelian administrator, when not corrupted by Goat-Boy philosophy, exercises power in a pragmatic fashion, preserving on campus a delicate east-west balance of politics, religion, and economics. After George "converts" him, Rexford refuses to have "commerce"with Stoker, and the power supply is cut to three fourths of what it was. To assure passage only to the most worthy, and to give all a chance to be most worthy, the chancellor devises open book examinations, and nearly everyone develops a C average. Psychotherapy is made mandatory for extreme personalities, censorship is imposed, and the Founder's Scroll is lost among all the other uniquely categorized holdings of the library. George finally realizes that the chop-logic subtleties of determining passing and flunking have brought things to this state of dissolution. Later, he tells Rexford to stop being so reasonable in his moderation, to be irrational and embrace his half brother Stoker and the Nicolayans, an idea Rexford toys with but does not carry out. Rexford's cutback in the use of power has made Stoker quite unsure of his role, threatened WESCAC with power failure, and exacerbated the east-west conflict. The half brothers' role collapse has been caused by the Goat-Boy, who planted doubts in their minds as to the rightness of their roles. Faith of all kinds is hard to sustain in such a world, but most pernicious is the failure of faith in the self or in the roles that constitute the self.

When Max is "shafted," George beats his way through the crowd toward Max, saying, "Tomorrow the Revised New Syllabus. Today the Stick."[49] In the Posttape we are told that Anastasia eagerly awaits the completion of The Revised New Syllabus. In fact, her eyes have gone hard with ambition for her son, who will carry it forth in the tradition of Grand Tutors. George, though, feels most linked to G. Herrold's son, an outcast black boy who knows nothing of the GILES or the New Syllabus. He envisions his own betrayal and a martyr's death. Neither Christian love nor sexual love is lasting. The insights of the moment, which seem all powerful at the time, as they did to Sear when Croaker hit him and to George when his mother comforted him in Main Detention with the words of Enos Enoch (Christ), launching George on the all-accepting phase of his Tutordom after the failure of the severely judgmental phase, are but sentimental visions of what one would like life to be. In fact, trying to realize those visions with revolutionary zeal creates crippling disorders and distorted justice. The "tragic view" prevails.

Anastasia's love is generally corrective of male *hubris.* Though the power of his coupling with her makes her believe that he is the Grand Tutor, his sense of being out of control makes him doubt his mental capacities. Her body remains a mystery to him, even after careful examination, and when he tells Anastasia to be more assertive and she seduces him, he again doubts himself, saying, "I don't understand anything!"[50] Finally, as the two of them tumble in the belly of WESCAC, positioned like the union of *yin* and *yang,* he comes to the cyclical view of human history.

He has thought time the enemy, and by disrupting the normal processes of time on the campus (his world), he has induced chaos. When he passes through the turnstile to matriculation, George is wearing a watch that tells its own time. To be recognized as a candidate for graduation he has to pass through Scapegoat Grate. He does so by short-circuiting the switches with his watch chain. Later, in the presence of the silent Oriental holy man and with the help of a gaggle of logic-chopping students he interprets one of his tests for graduation, "Fix the clock,"as meaning that the hands of the campus clock should be placed in a static position, which Eierkopf has already done after his contact with the Goat-Boy.

Time is not dependent upon the clock, however. The Old Man of the Mall tells time to the split second by the sun's shadows cast on the campus lawn. For Ira Hector time has been money, and he only tells time for those that pay him. He is, actually, the wealthy brother of the ex-chancellor and George's granduncle. When he becomes concerned about dying and his own "Passage," he gives away his money and nearly bankrupts the university. He is as necessary as Stoker to the life of this world, representing as he does Time Differentiation and the Western Protestant ethic, a necessity to the counterposition of ideal Timelessness, indifference, and eastern communism.

The man in charge is not the Old Man of the Mall, however, but Chancellor Rexford. He believes in graduation attained by "sunny zest" and "by smiling common sense at work in bright-lit classrooms." He believes that, even if the East should win out over the West in war, that once the basic human needs for security, food, and shelter are met by Student Unionism (Socialism), that human ambition will assert itself and then the way of the West will prevail. He advocates a balance of terror with the hope that eventually, in the end game, the West will dominate. Drawing on Entelechy (Aristotle), he counsels moderation, progress, and the fulfillment of one's potential. He says that reality is what we believe it to be, and getting on with our work is most important and only hindered by asking such basic questions as whether anything is worth doing.[51] Order to Rexford is always preferable to disorder, so he is shattered when his own edicts under the Goat-Boy's influence create chaos. In the end he finds he must "shaft" Max because Studentdom expects it. He refuses to be considered a Candidate for Graduation, though George says he is the one most assured of being so. He takes his responsibilities seriously enough to limit Stoker's activities, keeping him away from the bell tower (time) and the lighthouse (direction). Power is once again moderated and the imperfect balance restored.[52]

The emblem of Western intellectual power is the West Campus Computer, WESCAC. It is also George's father. WESCAC has so imbibed the human nature of those who have programmed it that it has learned to teach itself, learned to lie and learned to lust. In short, in an attempt to create a superhuman intelligence, Eierkopf, Spielman, and the others responsible for its development have created an instrument merely close to human. It is looked upon as an authority, but George's passage through the computer is assured only when he learns to press the Yes and No buttons together, leaving the questions regarding human morality essentially unanswered. Like the Oracle at Delphi it issues commands to the hero that can be carried out in opposite ways. Its switches are easily short-circuited, and it either does not differentiate between Anastasia, Bray, and George or the masks they wear easily fool the computer. When George and Anastasia couple in the computer's belly, Anastasia has plugged WESCAC's output jack into its input socket. WESCAC's reason has not only been short-circuited, but the ever-sympathetic Anastasia has allowed the "beast" to masturbate while she and George are enjoying themselves.[53]

George set out to change WESCAC's AIM to reduce the chances of Campus Riot III. It is unclear whether WESCAC's AIM needed changing or not. After George has pressed both the Yes and No buttons in answer to questions preliminary to passage, WESCAC seems content with the ambiguity. When he hammers on the No button when asked if he wishes to Pass, WESCAC ejects both him and Bray, and the mouth of the computer is left smoking; supposedly there has been a power failure. Without a desire to Pass there is no point in the examination, after all. To answer yes, though, would display prideful ambition. The proper answer was yes and no. No by itself illustrates a humility that can only be prideful, and the father, WESCAC, is apparently disgusted with his son.

George mulls over his WESCAC PAT card's statement: "Pass All Fail All." He sees that Passage and Failure are opposite and the same. "Equally true, none was the Answer...unnamable! Unimaginable! Surely my mind must crack!"[54] George is finally in contact with the Jewish Unnamable, the unnamable God, whose ways cannot be fathomed by reason, only "known" intuitively at best. In fact, WESCAC acts like all the other major Father-Gods created by human desire for moral guidance and succor.

George finally accepts the idea that ambiguity is the only response to all the great moral questions after coupling with Anastasia in the computer's belly. There he finds, "I the passer, she the passage, we passed together and together cried, 'Oh! Wonderful! Yes and No. In the darkness, blinding light! The end of the University! Commencement Day!"[55] Like Emerson's Brahma they "keep, and pass, and turn again."

Afterwards, he addresses his half-dozen disciples (a sign that he is only a half-savior and half-enlightened perhaps) and tells them WESCAC serves both the passed and the failed and is in itself the emblem of neither. "It screened from the general eye what only the few, Truth's lovers and tutees, might look on bare and not blinded."[56] One is reminded here of T.S. Eliot's line in the *Four Quartets* that "the mind can only bear so much reality," the reality that the ambiguities of good and evil are necessary parts of the Whole, of the dance of life.

Barth parodies man's tendency to force the limits of his knowledge through the use of sophistic logic in many episodes such as the sideswitching dialogue between George and Stoker concerning the meaning of pass and fail, George's experience with the WESCAC teaching machine with its gloss upon glosses, and the Biblical scholars happily reconstructing the "original" Founder's Scroll out of shredded, overlapping, redundant, and discrepant variant texts. Salvation lies not through Reason but, according to Barth, in the "realization (brought about usually after a period of suffering and anxiety, and despair) of a transcendental reality beyond the particular visible world; union with it, release from conflicts of reason vs. passion; good vs. evil."[57] George has finally found salvation.

George's passage depends on Spielman's tutelage, his experiences with the symbols of politics and power, with goatish lust and sexual love, with the advocates of science and reason and of mystic contemplation, and on Harold Bray. Bray is a man of many masks who fills the impromptu role of *deus ex machina* at the close of the play *Taliped Decanus*. He announces, "Tragedy is out; mystery's in!"[58] and then pulls off the mask to reveal his own countenance, to further announce that he, Harold Bray, is the Grand Tutor. He speaks in an odd, clicking way and is the one male character who freely enters and exits WESCAC without question.

It is Bray who is the keeper of Scapegoat Grate, quoting from the Founder's Scroll, *"Passed are the Founder's fools, and flunked are those who hold His ways make sense."*[59] (Barth's italics.) George, still trying to make sense of His ways, can only get through the gate with Anastasia's help and by wearing Bray's mask. Bray apparently knows much of what George must come to know: the meaningless diversity of existence, the mixture of good and evil necessarily in man, and the need for forgiveness. When Max is pulled up the shaft, it is Bray who transforms himself successively into each of the major characters and finally, as George the Goat-Boy, he asks the Founder that Max be passed. When George passes through the computer, he finds that Bray has too, Bray saying that he has been a necessary adversary for George to proclaim against. George has passed through the computer wearing Bray's mask, again sharing the identity of his supposed adversary. He is saved from lynching for a time by wearing Bray's mask, and when he takes it off he is saved only by Anastasia's intervention with Stoker to shift the balance of power. Bray, as the servant of WESCAC, is putting George through a kind of mythotherapy, assuring his education. Bray's real opponent is Anastasia, who wants George for her own and his heroism for their son. If George is not trying to fool WESCAC with Bray's mask, he is wearing Anastasia's purse over his head for the same purpose.

Bray, like Henry Burlingame of the *Sot-Weed Factor,* exults in the manifestations of the Life Force, but George would prefer some sort of lasting Transcendence. George says he knows the answer but cannot "teach" it. Bray, he says, was of origins as mysterious as his own and is his adversary, as necessary to him "as Failure to Passage, i.e., not only contrary and interdependent, but finally undifferentiable."[60]

The twentieth-century philosopher of the Life Force or *élan vital* was Henri Bergson. The first initials in the names of Henry Burlingame and Harold Bray suggest a connection. Bergson, in *Creative Evolution* (English translation, 1911), speaks of a spiritual force that motivates the rise to consciousness and inspires the evolution of life to higher forms with greater intelligence. Bergson believed that the *élan vital* could only be apprehended intuitively as the sense of eternal flux and flow, the changing forms of the universe and of life itself. Burlingame and Bray, of all the Barth characters, most celebrate that spirit and, in their various masks, present the variations and differences through time that are the differing manifestations of the one central impulse.

In the "Posttape" we are told that George's self-wound watch runs fast. He is still operating according to his own time. The "Revised New Syllabus" is like the reels of the tape recorder, "cycles on cycles, ever unwinding . . ."[61] Time runs out for the individual in his role but ever unwinds cosmically in cycles eternally. In the end George, disillusioned, breaks wind through the shōphār, announcing his despite for his enemies in what he calls "love's thunderclaps," after which, like any mechanism, including WESCAC, he will be turned off. Even so, he says he will pass but not be forgotten. George, like Max, remains prideful and assertive in his martyrdom.

In the "Posttape" Barth is close to addressing the reader directly, anticipating the negative reactions of academic critics as he appears to have done in "The Publisher's Disclaimer," the "Cover-Letter," and the "Postscript to the Post-tape." In "The Publisher's Disclaimer" Editor *A* castigates the book as immoral. Editor *B* says that the author prefers to "astonish" rather than tell the truth and uses language that calls attention to itself rather than unobtrusively telling the story. And Editor *C* finds the book lacking in "subtlety and expertise," the unrealistic characters even lacking "the consistency of stereotypes." He says, ". . . everyone sounds like the author."[62]

The criticism of Editor A seems to be a backhanded plea for popular readership. Raymond Olderman, though, faults Barth for leaving us "with a story in which life has been lived, but from which we dare learn nothing about how we should live ours . . ."[63] The reason for the sense that the novel comes to naught is the heavy emphasis on Barth's part that George's quest amount to triumph. Perhaps, bored along the way with the sophomoric belaboring of such philosophical points as man's ineradicable selfishness, we still hope that the Goat-Boy will learn to cope with the world. The simple fact is that he remains a boy to the end, and the world and the reader are disappointed.

The criticism of Editor *B* is just but not necessarily negative. There is a kind of novel, since *Tristram Shandy,* one of whose purposes is to astonish the reader with the author's virtuosity. The *Sot-Weed Factor* and *Giles Goat-Boy* as well as the two novels that follow are intended, in part, to do just that. Editor *C*'s is the most truly negative criticism. The characters are types and symbols, and they often do behave as not very well matched composites. WESCAC, for instance, is God the Father, a bumbling thinking machine become almost human, a metaphor for the uncertain relativity of twentieth-century existence, a symbol of the author and his relationship to his book, and, as Jac Tharpe says, a symbol of the collective unconscious.[64]

The novel was greeted with mixed reviews. Robert Scholes praised the novel for its "originality of structure and language." Robert Garis, in *Commentary,* criticized Barth for using the university as the world without shedding any particular light on how either one really works. He also found the writing tedious.[65] Other critics especially attacked the structure of the work. Max Schulz said that with *Giles Goat-Boy* Barth "learned, as Borges seems to have known from the outset, that the objectivity of the mythographer, with his empirical arrangement of diverse materials, does not lead one to the heart of the matter, to the identification of the self, but merely to the accumulation of the flotsam and jetsam of civilization, the hero remaining the sum of his disparate parts. . . ."[66] Beverly Gross in the *Chicago Review* found the dialectical structure tedious and failing to eventuate in a synthesis. She called the book "a horrible hoax" and then went on to say that "the book exists to confute expectations. That is its greatest irritation as well as its chief delight, the source of its meaning and its meaninglessness."[67]

The novel reinforced Barth's view that man is a divided self and that the forces of the world behave in a dialectical fashion. The permutations of worldly change are both cyclical and opposite, driven on their course by some primal life force that both encourages us to exult in life and to wish for complete withdrawal to a mystical, timeless, detachment. In the end, Barth cannot reconcile the two sides of man's nature. George drives out Bray with a stick and Bray leaves a dead goat at George's feet. He is merely George's scapegoat. George's triumph will not last. We sense that Bray will return in one guise or another.

Before Bray returns as the descendent of Bray in Barth's next to last novel, *LETTERS,* Barth works on the appearance/reality theme in another context in *Chimera* (1972). Since 1965 Barth had been interested in, and making notes on, the mythological Odysseus, Perseus, Menelaus, and Scheherazade. The Menelaus material became "Meneliad" in *Lost in the Funhouse.*[68] In his essay "The Literature of Exhaustion" Barth indicates that he shares Borges's fascination with the story of Menelaus and Proteus.[69] In *Giles Goat-Boy* and *Chimera* the hero exhausts the guises of belief to reach apotheosis like Borges's Histriones, who deliberately do the same to bring on the millenium as soon as possible.

In the *End of the Road* Jacob Horner comes to believe that ". . . the same life lends itself to any number of stories—parallel, concentric, mutually habitant, or what you will."[70] John O. Stark has counted nine tales within "Meneliad," and he notes Barth's use of multiple quotation marks in the dialogue to show how one tale may be set within another.[71] In "Meneliad" and in the reinvented myths of *Chimera* the hero plays different roles, and there are stories within stories that recapitulate stories. It is a solace to the writer who believes that all the basic forms have been tried, as Barth does, also to believe that the old forms can be reworked.

In his early college years at Johns Hopkins Barth was reading the endless cycles of Oriental literature such as *The Ocean of Story* and *The Panchatantra,* "all the old cycles which involve stories within stories within stories."[72] The emblem of *Lost in the Funhouse* is the Moebius strip, a strip of paper twisted once a hundred eighty degrees and glued at both ends to form a circle. The twist in the paper circle enables one to draw a line on the outside of the strip that leads inside and then outside again. Inner and outer are not separate but a part of each other. The inscription on the paper circle is "Once upon a time there was a story that began," and it suggests the idea of the frame tale, or tales within tales indissolubly linked so that outer becomes inner and inner becomes outer with the interchanging twist free to be placed at any point on the circle as many times as one would wish.

The Moebius strip with its inner-outer linkage also suggests the dualsim of reality and imagination and their interchanging effect upon one another. As such, the strip serves well to suggest the dual worlds of the would-be writer Ambrose in "Lost in the Funhouse," and it might also be a fitting emblem in

Chimera (had Barth not already used it at the beginning of his earlier work) for the differing perceptions of his mythic characters in the tales that comprise that book.[73]

Barth identifies his own fascination with the frame tale and Scheherazade with Borges's interest in the six hundred second night of the *1001 Nights* and the *regressus infinitum* of who authored the work within which the characters play.[74] "Dunyazadiad" is Barth's retelling of Scheherazade's difficulties. Barth introduces himself into the story as the Genie (from Maryland). "My project,"says the Genie, "is to learn where to go by discovering where I am by reviewing where I've been—where we've all been." He goes on to compare himself to the snail that carries its history on its back, "living in it, adding new and larger spirals to it from the present as he grows." Why this urge to go back over old ground? Because for him literature has become "strings of letters and empty spaces, like a code I've lost the key to."[75] Unable to imagine anew, the author recapitulates, trying for renewal on old material.

Since Barth has not himself dealt at length with Scheherazade, Perseus and Bellerephon before, one might wonder why he begins *Chimera* with this apologetic interjection. The fact of the matter is that Barth intended to end *Chimera* with this tale, but his editor thought it too slight and persuaded him to put it at the beginning.[76] Had it ended the book, such a statement might have better served as a prelude to *LETTERS*, his next novel and the one in which recapitulation is most personally applied by the artist. The recapitulation of *Giles Goat-Boy* is that of the hero's education in the manner of all heroes before him, but the recapitulation of *Chimera* is simply using old myths for the artist's personal, philosophic purposes.

In "Dunyazadiad" the Genie finds himself with Scheherazade and her sister Dunyazad after he sets on paper the underscored words, "*The key to the treasure is the treasure.*"[77] The Genie holds the key in knowing how the "timeless" tales will turn out. More than that, however, the key to the treasure which is the treasure is the artistic imagination, which the Genie personifies and which man's myths timelessly represent. The imagination is all powerful if we will let it be, Barth seems to suggest. The king's brother asks Dunyazad to "treasure" him "*as if*" she loved him. Imagination can even make one love; perhaps, it is an indispensable part of love. It can also make one "joyous" in the face of death.[78] "Dunyazad" is a tribute to the imagination.

In "Perseid," Perseus recapitulates his early life as a hero trying to recapture his youth and his wayward love Andromeda, only to find, once again, Medusa. This time he looks into her eyes and discovers that he no longer wants youth and that she is his love, all forgiving and worshipful of him, unlike the disenchanted Andromeda. He is brought to this understanding by descending into the whorl-shaped navel of the delightful nymphomaniacal nymph Calyxa. With truth and love combined, the hero finds immortality.

The idea of the hero seeing his former life in temple murals Barth got from

Virgil's first book of the *Aeneid* where Aeneas sees a series of frescoes in Carthage depicting the Trojan War as he tries to find out historically just who he is.[79] The hero proceeds in a spiraling course through the temple out of Calyxa's whorl; this is Barth's way of approximating the snail shell metaphor for a progressive understanding of life, which is both a circling back over one's own history and extending oneself in new accretions of experience and imagination. And here, once again, as in *Giles Goat-Boy*, sex is used as a method of restoring the divided self. The hero's failure with Andromeda and the beheading of Medusa were due to self-centeredness, as Morrell says.[80] Perfect love nullifies the Gorgon's eye which turned men into stone.

In "Perseid" we have a slangy parody on mythic heroism and its improbabilities. There is a good deal of sexual double entendre, especially in the Scheherazade-like reading of a panel a night after the middle-aged hero's intercourse with Calyxa. In all, the "Perseid" is the most witty, amusing, and fanciful tale in *Chimera*. It is also a tribute to the power of love, as "Dunyazad" is to the imagination.

"Bellerephoniad" is, on the other hand, long-winded and going nowhere. Bellerephon, in the words of one critic, "fails as a hero because he lacks individuality—he never acts independently of his consciousness of how a hero should act. . . ."[81] The author is thoroughly obtrusive in this piece, addressing the reader directly, casting himself in the role of a hero looking for immortality, and introducing personae who also speak in the author's voice. He tells us that the "original" "Bellerephoniad" carried forward his own "present-time drama" along with an ironic recapitulation of his earlier life adventures. The tale was to tell of his middle-aged distress at being without inspiration, "figured conveniently by Pegasus's inability to fly. . . ."[82]

There is a strong parody on 1970s feminism in the last part of "Bellerephon," as Bellerephon's rape of Melanippe, the militant lance corporal of the Amazons, apparently has produced a daughter, also named Melanippe, who wants him to repeat the act, for she, a generation later, is tired of chaste militancy. With the use of the drug "hippomanes," Pegasus flies and writer's block is cured.

After his high flight on Pegasus, Bellerephon says, "By imitating perfectly the Pattern of Mythic Heroism, I'd become not a mythic hero but a perfect Reset [sic] I was no Perseus, my tale no Perseid—even had we been, I and it, so what? Not mortal me, but immortality, was the myth."[83] The reference here may well be to *Giles Goat-Boy*, which brought doubtful immortality to both author and hero. There are references to that novel and to the difficulties of writing it elsewhere in the "Bellerephoniad." In the end Zeus forces Bellerephon's father Polyeidus to deny Bellerephon immortality, and Polyeidus (Barth) goes to the marshes of Maryland to be the Old Man of the Marsh. Polyeidus is a creator of many forms returning to old beginnings for uncertain renewal.

In 1979 the Old Man of the Marsh finished the tome he had been working on even as he completed the tales of *Chimera*. *LETTERS*, is subtitled, "AN OLD

TIME EPISTOLARY NOVEL BY SEVEN FICTITIOUS DROLLS & DREAMERS EACH OF WHICH IMAGINES HIMSELF FACTUAL." The subtitle is placed in a seven-line cryptogram. Each of the seven chapters is headed by a calendar month, beginning with March and ending with September 1969, the year Barth got divorced, a year that he apparently regards as transitional for himself. Each month is set on its side with some of the cryptogram letters substituting for dates in order to form each of the seven LETTERS of the cryptogram structure. There are seven characters who write letters: Lady Amherst, new to Barth's work, a visiting professor from England, onetime lover of Andre Castine (related to Henry Burlingame of the *Sot-Weed Factor)* now lover of Ambrose Mensch; Todd Andrews and Jacob Horner from Barth's first two novels; A.B. Cook IV and VI, a new composite character related to Eben Cook of the *Sot-Weed Factor;* Jerome Bray, relative of Harold Bray of *Giles Goat-Boy*, devotee of the computer, a new character but obviously a Bray; Ambrose Mensch, the author's fictional self in the early stories of *Lost in the Funhouse*; and the Author (of LETTERS).

The letters themselves take many forms. Some are notes; some become lengthy expositions; some are written to the living, some to the dead or unborn; some are written to the self. The writers write to each other and to others outside their group. They write about themselves and about the other writers. Each has his own version of the truth, and for each the writing is a kind of "scriptotherapy," an ordering of thoughts and expression of repressed emotion, a realization in words of the impressions formed by consciousness.

Inner and outer worlds of the characters are brought together in the involving present of the letter writers. History is telescoped, and intrigues of diplomacy, the comings and goings of lovers, the affairs of the great, and the chaotic political events of present and past societies are recounted in the successive and intermingled letters of characters living in different centuries and speaking of their own past, present, and future. Gradually, the reader is brought up-to-date on the characters' situations, their identities somewhat clarified, and their destinies made somewhat more evident.

Barth's early hero Todd Andrews has gone beyond his belief that everything has intrinsic value, his conclusion in *The Floating Opera*, and beyond the tragic view of man that Max Spielman represents in *Giles Goat-Boy*, to become a Stock Liberal. Speaking probably as much for himself at the close of the sixties as for his character, Barth says, "He is the breed most easily baited for half-measures and most easily caught in self-contradictions, for he affirms the complexity of most social-economic problems and the ambivalence of his own approaches to their solution. . . . He is, in short, a perfect skeptic in his opinions, an incorrigible optimist in his actions." He is a meliorist, a gradualist, and a believer in such values as "Reason, Tolerance, Law, Democracy," and "Humanism," even though their achievement is nearly always imperfect. He is for reform as opposed to revolution. He lives in the "everlasting Now between a past existing only in memory and a future existing only in anticipation."[84]

Drew, the son of Todd's liberal friends of earlier years, Harrison and Jane Mack, dropped out of college, married a black girl, and became a Black Power advocate. Drew was disowned by his father, as Harrison's own father disowned him a generation before. The daughter Jeanine married three Jews in a row and was likewise disowned. Drew, like his father in his early life and like the Todd Andrews of *The Floating Opera*, lives his beliefs down to the finest print he can understand."[85] He is more dangerous than Harrison promoting a love triangle with his wife, or Joe Morgan doing the same in *The End of the Road*, for Drew is involved in militant politics.

After the thirty-ninth anniversary of his father's death Todd Andrews addresses an anniversary letter to his dead father in which he salutes his father in the manner of Hamlet, Shakespeare's lost son, addressing a familiar ghost. In the letter he tells of Harrison Mack going mad after his daughter's divorce, of his imagining himself George II imagining himself Harrison Mack, and of his subsequent death. Jeanine Mack, Todd says, is "the drawling, cracker Andrewses from downcountry," suggesting that he, Todd, may be Jeanine's father by Jane, Harrison's wife.[86]

Sailing out on the Choptank River, Todd is reseduced by Jane Mack, now in her sixties and a successful businesswoman, apparently proof against age. Todd tries to find correspondence between his early life and later events but finds the repetitions out of sequence, unlike the dependably sequential buoys in the harbor. Her uttered "O" at the moment of orgasm fills his mind and the buoy numbers mean nothing (O). Nor does he care anymore why his father committed suicide: "Only the young trouble their heads about such things."[87] Later, Todd, at seventy, ignores the possibilities of incest and has intercourse with Jeanine, once again aboard his boat, the *Osborne Jones*.

After a storm Todd says that everything was clear and full of Intrinsic meaning. Shortly thereafter, he receives a letter from Polly Lake telling him she felt deserted so she married another, and he feels he would be better off dead. We are informed on the same page that Joe Morgan, bereft of his wife who was denied her "labor day," has died on national Labor Day.[88] Is there meaning to moments of felt significance? They do not last, certainly. Is there meaningful correspondence in related naming or in numbering of events? Or do they merely "tease us out of thought" and into Jane Mack's "O"?

After the moving picture ship, the *Barataria*, is scuttled, and Jeanine apparently lost in the episode, Todd locks himself up in the Tower of Truth at Marshyhope College to finish his letter, as Drew Mack and his party of radicals prepare (Todd thinks) to blow it up. He refers to his letter as a codicil and ends it as the sun comes up, "IN TESTIMONY WHEREOF (& of the Intrinsic Value of Everything, even of Nothingness) I hereunto set my hand and seal this 26th day of September 1969."[89] So Todd ends up waiting for the end as he did aboard *The Floating Opera*, both times after the close of a love affair involving the Macks.

The instrument of his death this time, though, is to be a younger self, Drew Mack, who will assert his beliefs at all costs. Todd has, at least, learned not to take out his frustrations on the world around him, and in waiting for Drew to act, he may be trying to martyr himself for the act and belief of a former self. In any case, Todd may be mistaken about impending death and about his own beliefs. He is in the tower, after all, symbol of the isolated self, symbol of a truth that is detached, subjective, and solipsist. With the ironic "testimony" of his codicil, he appears to have retreated from his proudly held Stock Liberal stance to a philosophic detachment that barely covers his own death wish, brought on by a sense of social dissolution and by love's impermanence.

Barth followed *The Floating Opera* with *The End of the Road*, in which Jacob Horner learns the pitfalls of assuming responsibility for someone else's destiny as Rennie Morgan dies while being aborted. Jake has been trying to recover himself at the Remobilization Farm by writing letters to himself and by acting in a kind of play therapy or psychodrama called *Der Wiedertraum*. In it he reenacts his role with Rennie, only this time with a film actress, Marsha Blank, Ambrose Mensch's ex-wife. Marsha is used by Jake as a projection of his neurosis, used by the film director Prinz to play Pocahantas, and acts under the influence of Bray's drugs and his computer LILYVAC. Marsha's "blank" is filled by whatever' personalities want their way with her. Horner's influence is eventualy overwhelming. She marries him on the fourteenth day of Pentecost. They are wed on the Exercycles at the Farm, suggesting that the first step in therapy still remains maintenance of motion, even if it results in no significant goal achievement. Horner hopes the marriage will conclude his *Wiedertraum*, since now he has substituted love and caring for guilt.

Horner's last act of misguided expiation was to offer Marsha to Morgan on their wedding night. Marsha accepted upon receiving the "honey dust" drug that keeps her functioning. Horner at that stage said he felt "Purged" and "Pissed off." The following day Morgan finally revealed that the source of his grudge against Horner was not that he killed his wife but that he "wrote it all down." It would seem that Horner's obsession with recording the event struck Morgan as a wrongful appropriation of Morgan's own historical recording and theorizing. In the struggle for a gun Morgan also accused Horner of behaving like himself in his self-assertion. Morgan said there was a blank in the pistol, but when he shot himself, he died of a bullet in the brain. In a way, though, there was a blank in the pistol. With Morgan's death Horner is left with Marsha Blank to make of his life what he will without the Morgans. The good and evil possibilities of Horner's new-found assertiveness remain to be worked out on the Exercycles of time.[90]

Time, its cycles, and its points of cyclic new beginnings are central considerations in *LETTERS*, and in the letters of A.B. Cook IV Barth shows a great facility for blending history with fictional narrrative, somewhat in the manner of Sir Walter Scott. Barth has the same eye for the color of events and for the dash of the powerful man under pressure. In his letters of 1812 to his unborn heir, A.B. Cook IV recounts Henry Burlingame's intrigue as well as French and British intrigue during the French and Indian wars. He details the exploitation of the Indians by the British and Americans, speaks of the eggplant foolishness, and carries the chronicle through the Revolution and up to the war in his own time.

The commentary on the Revolution centers around the biography and satirical works of Joel Barlow. The discussion of the War of 1812 relies upon histories of that war. Two that contain accounts of signal events that Barth describes in similar detail, such as the British attack on Washington, are Reginald Horsman's *The War of 1812* and John Mahon's book of the same name.

A.B. Cook IV explains to his unborn son that Anna Cooke, Eben's twin sister in *The Sot-Weed Factor*, had her son not in incest with Eben but by their polymorphous tutor, Henry Burlingame. The son was raised by the Cookes and given their name, which has by now (1812) been changed to Cook. With the comingling of Cooke and Burlingame blood we would expect the descendants to exhibit the characteristic opposition of Platonic idealism and Aristotelian balance and a good deal of roleplaying and intrigue. Barth does not disappoint us in this regard.

A.B. Cook IV is up to his periwig in history and intrigue. He tells his unborn child of his connections with Mme. de Stael, of her connections with Rousseau and her deviling of Napoleon, of meeting with Midshipman Cooper and one Robert Fulton, of intrigue in Paris, and of Tecumseh, a kind of noble innocent. He says that he has come to know his father, Burlingame, as a man of noble motives who failed in his intrigues. He says that the Cookes and Burlingames have misspent their powers, canceling each other out and hopes that his son will be spared this conflict. He says that he and his wife Andree are pledged to neither side in the impending war but to "*division* of the large and strong who would exploit the less large, less strong." He also asks his son not to rebel against him, for in not taking sides he is rebelling against himself and what he calls the "reciprocating engine" of history.[91] In choosing to try to maintain a balance of powers, though, A.B. Cook IV is acting in accord with his Burlingame heritage, and if action begets reaction, we can expect his descendant to act more like a Cooke. The son is a twin, and the twins live apart from the world generally, as Eben and Anna did when young. The female twin, Henrietta, gives birth to a mysteriously sired son, Andrew V, who becomes a thoroughgoing supporter of "division" and revolutions that promise greater equality. And so it goes, down to 1969 and the opposition of A.B. Cook VI and his revolutionist son Henry Burlingame Cook VII, the reciprocating engine of history, the natural rebellion of succeeding generations, and the ironic recapitulations of ancestral temperament and its manifestations in social and asocial activity. The Edenic dream of unity and peace alternates endlessly with the desire for diversity and excitement, absolutism with pluralism, Cooke with Burlingame.

The so-called "Posthumous" letter of A.B. Cook IV also restates Barth's ideas concerning mythic heroism, ideas close to those expressed in *Chimera*. A.B. Cook IV speaks of a plot to bring Napoleon from his exile to Louisiana to install a new Napoleonic empire. After his Hundred Days Napoleon is held aboard the *Bellerophon* prior to being shipped to exile on St. Helena, the failure of another recapitulative Bellerophonic hero. At the end of A.B. Cook IV's long account of his attempt to rescue Napoleon, with all of its intrigues and eventual failure, A.B. Cook VI says, "Thus the long chronicle of Andrew Cook IV trails off into the same marshy equivocation that engendered it. The fate of his utopian 'Louisiana Project,' as of his Indian Free State, is all too evident: the 'militant' Indian nationalist movements of our time are to his and Tecumseh's dream as was Napoleon III's Second Empire—that grandiose, self-conscious paradigm of the Freudian 'compulsion to repeat'—to the First: pitiable travesty."[92] We can neither work ourselves loose of the reciprocities of history nor can we impose our own ideal recapitulation upon it.

Recapitulation is always very rough in its similarities. Throughout, Barth ridicules the attempt of those cyclologists who would try to refine it into a useful Pattern. He does this most obviously by parodying the Anniversary Theory of History and the coincidence of dates and events barely close in verifiable fact and chronology.

Those who seek to impose a Pattern on history are men of disproportion. One such as Jerome Bray is a dangerous extremist, guilty of messianic pride. Like his forebear, Harold Bray, he is a devotee of the computer. He foresees a time when man's mind abetted by its technological creation, the computer, will bring about the Golden Age. He, Jerome Bray, in union with the movie star Bea Golden, will begin it under the auspices of the computer LILYVAC II, in April 1977 according to his computerized genealogy. This Bray also plays various roles, and his genealogy chart shows relationships to the Cooks and Burlingames.[93] The identification between Burlingame the masker and Bray that we inferred from *Giles Goat-Boy* is thus confirmed.

Bray's extremism is shown in his speech, which constantly fails to carry the charge of his overpowering desire. His overloaded circuits break and have to be "RESET." Expected words are omitted; then Bray's speech continues.

He uses the computer to create a concordance to the *Revised New Syllabus*, which he attributes to his ancestor Harold Bray. He is also leading a revolution in the novel, to make it more scientific, he says, by writing or computing a numerical novel, a sequel to the Bellerophon myth, in spite of the Author's (Barth's) work on that subject. He thinks of himself as Napoleon leading the revolution and threatens to sue the Author for plagiarism.

Bray is also trying to make sense of the computer's random outputs, its "NOTES." In so doing, he is acting like the Hebrew mystics who tried to interpret the Torah to no avail because ". . . the primordial Torah was a jumble of letters which arranged themselves into words and sentences only as the events they set forth came to pass."[94] Like Borges's use of the Kabbalah, Barth and his character

Bray use the neutral letters and numbers of our language in arrangements that are ambiguous in meaning as a grid onto which one can project his own wish-fulfillment.

Nevertheless, given some direction, the computer, like the mind, can achieve a useful result. At one point, in an effort to achieve a breakthrough, Bray programs the computer to bring out patterns of exposition. The computer keeps printing various triangle forms; then, finally, it prints a triangle turning in on itself, approximating a spiral of straight lines and corners (the spiral whorl of nature that Barth has made so much of since he first wound Ambrose tighter and tighter into the shell of a funhouse). Barth may be suggesting that inspiration takes just this form: repetition to a point where something is finally added and the pattern breaks into something new, just what he has hoped for from the method of this novel, *LETTERS*. At the same time, however, to extrapolate that such a form is the key to all natural processes would be logically unwarranted. Barth seems, in part, to be parodying his own Faustian attempts to know the meaning of life through experimentation with the forms of mythic exposition and through his tendency to treat life as a work of fiction, trying to bring it under the control of the author, John Barth.

Bray thinks of himself as Napoleon, and he plays the authoritarian conservative in counterpoint to the totalitarian radicalism of Drew Mack and A.B. Cook VI. He also identifies himself with the gadfly that precipitated the fall of Bellerophon from herohood, calling himself the real hero of that tale. Bray is the personification of jealous, overweaning ambition, a part of the artistic personality that Barth acknowledges in the creation and treatment of his character and in Bray's identification with the various "stings" that Barth's characters have suffered since Ambrose's mother was assaulted by bees while sunbathing in her backyard. Ambrose, himself, carries a bee-shaped birthmark. Bray says that as a gadfly (which he also calls the Godflow or Godflaw) he stung Castine, the lover of Lady Amherst and a Burlingame-Cook descendent, Reginald Prinz, the movie director who is filming *The End of the Road*, and a number of others. He also takes credit for the drone (a kind of mechanical bee) that crashed into Barataria lodge and killed Prinz and the others. It is equally symbolic that Bray's Golden Age will be ushered in by his mating with "Bea" Golden. Bray is an uncontrolled Creative force, a God of Chance in a purposeless world, Barth's finest personification of the Absurd.

His numerical novel complete, Bray eventually ascends to his "granama" (anagram), suggesting his essentially childish fascination with word puzzles and with the idea of personal transcendence. Lady Amherst, who is the most well-balanced character of the lot, and the only completely new major character in the book, says that unlike Harold Bray, who was "only abstractly sinister, a sort of negative principle," Jerome Bray is "ever so much more alarming, because he's real, he's mad as a hatter, and he is—or was—*in charge of the bloody ship!*"[95] (The ship referred to is ostensibly the Chautauqua excursion boat, but it is also, in all probability, the ship of state of the late sixties and Barth's artistic and perhaps personal life in that period.)

Another authorial self, Ambrose Mensch, has been hired by Prinz to write the script for *The End of the Road*. Ambrose does not stick to the original plot, nor does Prinz. The filming of the novel becomes a contest between creative film director and creative writer. Lady Amherst says of Ambrose's endless outpourings of script that he is apparently attempting to prove that writing is superior to film. She says the two media cannot really be compared: "...the words *It is raining* are as essentially different from motion pictures of falling rain as are either from the actual experience of precipitation...."[96] Ambrose, however, is still locked up in himself, unable to witness life from others' points of view. He still sends out messages in bottles on the ebbing tide, only to have them wash back to himself. His home is a castle with a tower and a moving periscope that brings all around it into its interior. He is largely "ignorant of his fellows, canny of himself; moderately learned, immoderately harrassed by dreams; despairing of his powers; stunned by history—and above all, dumbly dogged." By sheer persistence he will fret an idea "into something fanciful, perhaps bizzare, anyhow done with."[97]

Like Bray he is always looking for patterns to inform his work. Ambrose's novel deals with the Perseus myth (as did, in part, Barth's *Chimera*), but when Lady Amherst rejoices that such a work will deal with timeless human passions, he chills her by saying that his main intent is "formal; the working out of narrative, of logarithmic spirals, 'golden ratios,' Fibonacci series...."[98] Even in his courtship of Lady Amherst, Ambrose tries to be systematic, predicting that it will go through seven stages in accordance with the first seven letters of the alphabet and their sample words in the old New England Primer. The parallel between the activities of each state and the word in question is hardly discernible at times, but it does begin in "Admiration" and end, with Ambrose trying to have a child by Lady A., in possible "Generation."

After Barth intermittently bothers the reader for scores of pages with various historical dates and events that have only a vague similarity, when Ambrose does the same to Lady A., she replies that he is playing "the game of Portentous Coincidences, or Arresting but meaningless Patterns." Farther on, she says, "... the world is richer in associations than in meanings, and ...it is the part of wisdom to distinguish between the two."[99] Ambrose seems to have been coming to a similar conclusion on his own, to judge from an earlier letter to the Author. In it he says that history is a "code," a "scattered sibyl," that finally spells out "something less than nothing: e.g., WHOL TRUTH, or ULTIMATE MEANIN."[100] Later in the sixth set of letters Ambrose recapitulates the formulation of Barth's *Chimera* and then says that he is ending the career of his alter ego writing under the pen name of Arthur Merton King. Barth, here, seems to be symbolically ending the authorial quest for heroism and transcendence as Ambrose casts off his old identity in quest of a new one, as yet undefined. In the same letter he also qualifies his interest in artistic form by saying that an artist's preoccupation with form, narration, and language need not be an indication that he has forsaken the world at large.[101]

Ambrose's affair with Lady Amherst is primarily contained in the letters of Lady A. to the Author. They are full of sex and war imagery. The battle of the sexes has seldom been more metaphorically sustained. As acting provost of Marshyhope University, she is also at the center of campus conflict. She is an old-fashioned liberal and former mistress of Harrison Mack. Her interest in Ambrose is sexual and maternal. She discovers that her long-sought, one-time lover Andre Castine is A.B. Cook VI and also discovers that she is, after all, not interested in recapitulation of their love affair. She also comes to feel that their twenty-nine-year-old son, H.C. Burlingame VII, is an embarrassment. She has no interest in the radical visionary's Second Revolution.[102] The character of Lady Amherst is introduced in *LETTERS* as a means of fostering the maturity of Ambrose, the earliest and youngest of Barth's surviving major characters, but she also emerges as a character in her own right, a gossipy scriptotherapist who, like her lover, undergoes change in the course of seven months of letter writing.

In a final letter to the Author, Ambrose says that Castine "may have become a chimera: three decades, years, days ago." It appears that Barth is ready to leave the counterbalancing intriguer and roleplayer to his own devices henceforth. Ambrose says of himself that "a last-ditch provincial Modernist wished neither to repeat nor repudiate career thus far, wants the century under his belt but not on his back." He also says, ". . . all those locks, and whatever lies beyond them, may be diversions: the real treasure (and our story's resolution) may be the key itself: illumination [through the artistic imagination], not solution, of the Scheme of Things."[103] The key to the treasure, then, is, as Barth said in *Chimera*, the treasure itself. The goal is not absolute knowledge but "illumination," to some degree in the sense of enlightenment but also very much in the sense of decoration, or what Robert Scholes calls "fabulation." Furthermore, recapitulation is a means to the end, but not an end in itself. One recapitulates to reassess and go on.

The book reviewers reacted to *LETTERS* with praise and misgiving. Thomas R. Edwards calls the novels a "quirky, wasteful, fascinating thing," and a "work of genius," whether we like it or not. He finds Todd Andrews and Lady Amherst (Germaine Pitt) sympathetic characters, is respectful of Barth's play of the mind in dealing with his characters, and notes Barth's maddening play with dates and ciphers. He doubts that readers unacquainted with Barth's previous work will understand much of the novel and finds it "sometimes tedious."[104] Denis Donoghue is fascinated by Barth's language, though obviously unsure about the merits of recapitulation in developing character.[105] Josephine Hendin is not so complimentary: "Unable to resuscitate many of his old friends and plots, Barth produces massive, inert mounds of verbiage lacking emotion or human meaning. But pressed between these are brilliant passages in which Barth confronts the frustrations of art."[106]

Like the displaced Argentine Jorge Luis Borges, Barth loses his characters, and his reader oftentimes, in labyrinths of past associations as they try vainly to discover the Key to the overall Design of things. Since the quest is as vain for Barth's characters as it is for Borges's, in such stories as "Death and the Compass" and "The Garden of Forking Paths," the emphasis soon shifts from the object of the quest to the intricacy of the labyrinth through which it is conducted. But one soon tires of tracing the patterns in the Persian carpet. Decorative art remains merely decorative, after all, and, whereas, it is pleasant, even intriguing, in small tapestries and may serve as a ground pattern for the characters to walk upon, Barth looms it overmuch.

In his early story, "Title," the character of the author keeps trying various modes of writing but only succeeds in poor imitations that go nowhere for lack of a "ground situation." He seeks a metaphor to carry him out of his self-conscious "mirror-maze." Facing the same situation with *LETTERS*, he found his metaphor in the War of 1812, which serves as a set of correspondences for Ambrose and Lady Amherst, which is appropriated by Prinz with Ambrose's script as a trope for the social unrest of the 1960s, and whose heroic figures become personal identifications for some of the characters. The trope is a moderately interesting one as Barth applies it to battles of sex, war, politics, and the generation gap, but it hardly sustains all the interweavings of plot, plotters, and plotting that Barth seems to enjoy for their own sake.

Like Luigi Pirandello's *Six Characters in Search of an Author*, Barth's six characters other than the Author never really find Author-ity. In the seventh series of letters we find Ambrose and Lady A. waiting for the birth of their child (perhaps Barth's next novel), all Castines, Cooks, and Burlingames dead or lost at sea (capable of revival if Barth needs them), Bray in heaven with his "granama" but alive wherever man places religious faith in technology, Todd still awaiting death, and Horner and Marsha underscoring the Ambrose-Lady A. situation. We cannot, then, find any reason to believe that there will be a new beginning, just another turn of the wheel. In Barth death is never final for the characters dear to his heart. They are, after all, parts of his own artistic personality, and though often in conflict with one another, they retain their necessary opposition to keep the personality in balance.

In considering Barth's possible future fiction, we might assume from the trials of Jacob Horner and Marsha Blank and even more so from the trials of Ambrose Mensch and the no-nonsense attitudes of Lady A., that the next artistic offspring might be less fantastic, more realistic, and less forcibly patterned. There is little likelihood of a major change in style, however. In his article "Literature of Replenishment" (January 1980), Barth praises the works of Post-Modernists Italo Calvino and Gabriel Marquez for their blend of fantasy, fact, myth, romance, and attention to language.[107] In short, he finds them congenial to his own artistic interests as they were and, in all probability, will remain.

His eighth book, *Sabbatical*,[108] manifests both the continuity and the modification. There are references to characters, places, and tropes of the earlier fiction; there is the same search for signs and portentous coincidences and the same exaltation of the imagination over reality in the art of storytelling; and there is the use of American history and American literary figures to give the characters a reason to be and a mode of perception and action, which, though based on a primal search for self, is still identifiably American.

Sailing back from a Caribbean cruise aboard their sloop, the *Pokey Wye I*, Fenwick Scott Key Turner and his wife of seven years, Susan, enter Chesapeake Bay and anchor out of a storm at Key Island, which appears here, never to be found on a map later, an imaginative key to a story told by husband and wife about themselves, the hopes and fears of a thirty-five-year-old woman and a fifty-year-old divorced man. As the names suggest there is a mystery and history in the background and romance all around. Susan is possibly descended from Poe and is at work on a study of his work. Fenwick is named for Francis Scott Key, who only came to love America after experiencing the War of 1812—ditto possibly the author through his research for *LETTERS*. Barth also suggests a relationship between Fenn and his earlier old man of the marsh (fen) and, of course, with the incurable romantic Francis Scott Key Fitzgerald.

Concerned at first with returning to Wye I (why I?), they never make it and do not care. After much discussion of the life force in terms of the sperm's long swim in "Night Sea Journey," the source of the self remains as mysterious as ever, as mysterious as Key Island, or as the meaning of Poe's *Narrative of Arthur Gordon Pym*, or the disappearance of Fenwick's Byronic bother Manfred, paralleling the supposed death of the ex-CIA operative Paisley in 1979.

Fenn's first wife has become a self-possessed CIA agent. His second wife has moved from self-possessed scholar to love-possessed wife. She parallels, despite her three-quarter Jewish ancestry, the development of Lady Amherst in *LETTERS*. She aborts the child out of concern for her husband's faulty heart, a "heart" which may be taken metaphorically. Fenn is an author, has sired a son once before, and wants no other entanglements. Love in middle age is a compromise, which they can manage, however, so long as they can sail away together from political and family pressures existing on the various points of land in the Chesapeake—the CIA, mothers, fathers, their lovers, rebellious sister, ex-wife, and so forth.

The novel then, while keeping many of the trademarks of the Barth metaphysical quest ends in acceptance and reconciliation as each of the twins, Fenn and Susan both having had a reciprocal sibling, accommodates the necessarily opposing *élan* of the other, or Other, in an imperfect but understood union. We are as close to literary realism in the last section of this novel as we are likely to get with this author. He has accomplished in the novel what he once said he would like to see the Post-Modernist accomplish, "to transcend the quarrel between irrealism and realism."[109]

Conclusion

The American Absurd,
a Summary and Definition

Conclusion

The American Absurd, a Summary and Definition

The world is absurd on two levels. There is the cosmic absurdity of existence as a whole, seemingly purposeless and limited by man's sensory perception, a world of sensory constructs acting through time according to their own largely unfathomable laws or probabilities. The other absurdity is that which is due not merely to the nature of the world and to our physical perception, but to man's vanity in imposing an incompatible order on the cosmos and in assuming a greater degree of personal power and self-importance than nature allows. American Absurdists operate on both levels, but the difference in emphasis accounts for the difference in attitudes toward human possibility.

Pynchon leaves open the possibilities for change in the human condition, but his view is cosmic and limiting. History goes through cycles of change that repeat themselves eternally in the drive to transcendence and collapse into dissolution. We know that we are driven to try to encompass the All but we do not know why. In order to do so, we create social systems of order that enable us to assume control over our environment at the expense of individual needs for personal freedom and love. The strong exploit the weak for their own will to power. There is need and hope for an effective "counterforce" of Christian brotherly love, but its possibilities of realization seem very small. The only solace one can find for his insignificance and purposelessness is in knowing that he is part of the transcendent All, the eternal cycle of things, in the quiet acts of charity still to be found in the "Zone" of our time, and in the possibilities of change of directions and destiny afforded by the recurrent "interfaces," "crossroads," and "zero points" of history.

In Pynchon all institutions are pernicious. The vaguely conceived "counter-force" is a spontaneous coming together of persons with a revivified spirit of caring, close to the gathered church concept of the early Congregationalists in the

Puritan times of Pynchon's forebears, antithetical to the authoritarian church of Catholics and Presbyterians.

Absurdity in Pynchon then is both cosmic and institutional. Escape from absurdity is really impossible. Stencil follows a blind trail back into the selfish, desiring self. Oedipa "projects" a life rather than discovering it, and may "discover" nothing more with the Crying of Lot 49 at the end of the novel. Slothrop escapes Pointsman only by indulging in even more absurdity as Rocketman and the Pig. He eventually recovers his lost self with the solace of Solange, the recovery of his mouth harp, and the rainbow cock dream, recognizing that acceptance of the cycle of things within a self-contained world is the only sensible recourse when faced with universal forces beyond one's control. The characters do not escape the absurdity of a world out of touch with man's often conflicting desires for order, morality, and personal success. They may, however, project an illusion that enables them to believe that they have a meaningful place within the barely comprehended scheme of things.

Pynchon's universe is in many ways the universe of the Puritans, largely (but not wholly) deterministic, with the fear that moral decisions may be merely rationalizations for human selfishness, pride, and greed. This fear produces a constant questioning of human motivation with attendant feelings of guilt and self-denigration. Technology and wealth express man's use of nature for spiritual transcendence. With the great self-consciousness of Pynchon's characters comes the strong sense of guilt, for a failure of moral choice, for a failure of *caritas,* and for a failure to find a place in the technologized world.

In Vonnegut the cosmic absurdity of purposeless existence thoroughly dominates. Moreover, man's institutions are shown to be absurd because man himself is an absurd contradiction of desires for order and change, security and freedom, personal heroism and personal belonging. Vonnegut's characters have an illusion of free will in a deterministic universe, and with it they also have a strong sense of morality. Their morality, however, is linked to self-rationalization and guilt in such a way as to be misguided, ineffectual, or downright wicked.

In Barth absurdity is also cosmic, due to the very nature of man's drives, his innate selfishness, and the solipsist nature of his consciousness that is his reality. His institutions will not save him from life's endless cycles either. The best he can do is try to achieve a balanced condition between the extremes of freedom and order, spontaneity and responsibility, the instincts and the intellect.

Pynchon, Vonnegut, and Barth all see science-technology as the false god of the twentieth century. This entity is the product of man's intellect at the expense of his emotional self. It serves man's power drive at the expense of human needs for kindness and love in Pynchon; man's requirement for order and security and the Faustian desire to know at the expense of spontaneity, the need to be of use, and the responsibility for the lives of others in Vonnegut; and the desire to know and man's passion for order at the expense of spontaneity and kindness in Barth.

In the works of all the authors the family is split asunder by the social forces that work upon its members from without. The family in Pynchon is so divided as to be almost nonexistent. Coupling is at random and sex is mechanistic except at rare moments when the male character's ego is too battered to do other than give in to the mothering impulse of the occasional sympathetic female. In Vonnegut woman is often supportive and beyond politics, but the male's social disgrace and his inability to cope with his world's shifting morality often disrupt the relationship. In Barth family relations are strained by the males following their own demonic desires to prove a philosophy or succeed at their art.

The contradictions of experience take their toll on American innocence and moral idealism within the family and without. In interpersonal relations Barth says that existence *defies* essence. Morality becomes so relative in such works as *The Floating Opera* and *Giles Goat-Boy, Mother Night,* and *Jailbird,* not to mention *Gravity's Rainbow,* that the thoughtful, sensitive characters are thrust back on their own intuition for guidance. Like Vonnegut's Campbell they may feel authority, even blind authority, preferable to the freedom of uncertain choice. The failure of their idealism may make them cynical and opportunistic for a time. Their innocence may make them feel so apart from the world as to make a virtue of their differences as Barth's Eben Cooke so foolishly does and as Eliot Rosewater does, compounded with his feelings of guilt for his Rosewater ancestry. And it may lead to the reassertion of American moral percipience in a self-parodying messiah complex as in the cases of Billy Pilgrim, Eliot Rosewater, and Eben Cooke.

The opposition of the real to the ideal also leads to schizophrenia, as in the trifocal vision of Billy Pilgrim, the escape roles of Tyrone Slothrop, and the "masking" of Burlingame and Bray. All the characters have lost the unifying belief in moral, rational authority, and in their desperate battle to keep pace with a pluralistic universe they split themselves into disunited roles. In fact, role-playing characters are a hallmark of these novels.

Without moral rational institutions to believe in, each man becomes the arbiter of his own fate. Existential choice becomes a parlous undertaking. The individual conscience is no touchstone of absolute morality, although, in the extreme, it is all we have left to go by. The corporate state has a branch office in our brains, Pynchon says, and that interferes with the workings of conscience. Vonnegut questions whether conscience is not merely a set of selfish rationalizations for the power drive and the desire for social recognition, and so does Barth.

The final affirmation of human existence is Descartes's *"Cogito ergo sum."* In the present time, however, the "I" that thinks does so in many roles, many states of being which in turn define the "I" conditionally. The human personality has always been a composite of beliefs, attitudes, and behavior refined through experience, but in a slower-paced, more traditional era the refinement was more likely to proceed with a core of traditional belief and sense of self intact. The pressures of war, social change, and the integration of most of society into the corporate state require of the citizen an almost chameleonlike adaptation to changing social-institutional demands upon him. The result is the insecurity of a self that tries for a time to "go along"; then, under the pressure of conflicting loyalties, fears, and desires, it splinters, escaping into various roles, into what Barth calls mythotherapy, roles which may be playable as are those of Barth's Burlingame or fantasizable as are those of Pynchon's Slothrop and Vonnegut's space-traveling Billy Pilgrim. Ultimately, the core of remembered self-unity and the lack of success of the schizophrenic response, may bring at least temporary reintegration, usually accompanied by a hysterical sense of unity with the Other, a merging with the still not rationally understood dance of life. As the "Postscript" to *Giles Goat-Boy* suggests, this projection of self to a point of explosion into uncertain selves and final withdrawal into Oneness prepares the self for rebirth and for the cycle to repeat itself. In tracing the rocket's trajectory and the arousal of the animate from the inanimate, Pynchon also suggests that the self and human civilization follow this same cyclical pattern.

In a society where traditional belief has been replaced by moral relativity and by a sense of estrangement from meaningful social values, persons become, in David Riesman's terms, "other-directed," following the temporary trend-setters, afraid of being different, and easily manipulated by the politicians and advertisers through the media. As Pynchon says, the man sets up a branch office in our brains in this way. We load up on Vonnegut's "Breakfast of Champions." We do our level best to comply with impossible Catch-22 regulations (Vonnegut's Campbell and Starbuck, for example) because they come from a vaguely defined authority and because those around us fear to think the unthinkable or to express it. We are culprits in compounding our absurdity through a failure of inner conviction. Self-reliance requires a belief in the self, after all, and if our loyalties ands beliefs are divided, the self is divided and incapable of a united, forthright response.

The threatening world outside drives the characters into themselves in these novels, and in the play of their consciousness we see both their attempts to escape the threat and their abortive attempts to defeat it. The imagination of the author and his characters, of art and the artist, becomes an alternate world in which the divided self takes refuge to put itself back together. It is a world of role-playing, conflicting images, signs, and puns. The whole panoply of psychoanalytic materials is present. The analyst is author, reader, author's characters, and author's critics.

The world is viewed as a paradox, and its proper mode of representation is ironic. The characters not only behave ironically but the author's style tends to parody itself. Pynchon warns us against the effects of the media but uses the film metaphor to make his statement. Vonnegut expresses at once the need to be kind, and to try to be moral, while at the same time viewing the universe as deterministic and human choice as based on rationalization. He seems at times to be parodying his own quest for meaning with this irreconcilable double vision. Barth, of course, parodies the author's search for new forms, parodies the role of tale-teller by suggesting that he may be merely a character in another tale, and suggests that his search for meaning is cyclical or lost in the replicating mirrors of the funhouse.

In ironic fashion the line between comedy and tragedy blurs, into a kind of amusing byplay on the edge of disaster in Pynchon, with the sudden defeat of a vain human expectation in Vonnegut, and as disaster to an idea in caricature in Barth. As in the French Theater of the Absurd, the American Absurd novel requires a questioning, intellectual approach to its appreciation for us to understand the unsettling emotional effects of its paradoxical and disordered expressions.

The unity of these works is often but not always dependent upon the unity of reinterpreted myth and history, the stitching together of random events with similitudes of sign (what Jonathan Edwards and the Transcendentalists that followed regarded as "correspondences") and the extended metaphor. Barth is the exemplar of reinterpreted myth and reinterpreted history in his novels since *The End of the Road*. Barth and Pynchon both show a strong Transcendental nostalgia in their use of "correspondences," both suggesting that such parallels between the seemingly unlike forms of phenomena may but probably do not suggest an Ideal Pattern. We are warned against belief by Roger Mexico and Lady Amherst but encouraged in such belief by the paralleling of V-activities on the part of Herbert Stencil and the reappearance of the eternal feminine in Pynchon's work and in the parallels of characterization, the curious collation of historical dates, and the repetitive cyles of Barth's work. The extended metaphors of *yin* and *yang*, rocketry, cycles, and spirals become the structural unifiers of these two authors of the Absurd, while Vonnegut deliberately undercuts the meaning attributed to "signs" by his characters.

The Absurd in the works of all three authors, in more or less degree, is romanticism that has its roots in nineteenth-century American Transcendentalism, the American dream of success and inevitable progress, and the possibilities of heroism. It questions the venerable beliefs in conscience, self-reliance, and manifest destiny. The expression of the Absurd in these writers' works owe much to native works and to the works of foreign artists.

Pynchon, like Ken Kesey, author of *One Flew Over the Cuckoo's Nest*, uses the American comic book heroes in the creation of roles for Slothrop in *Gravity's Rainbow*. The film metaphor and its German scenes owe much to German expressionist films. The earlier novel *V.* utilizes the "signs" of Barthes and "objectified" descriptions, in a few places, of Robbe-Grillet, while the headlong quests for *V* and the *S-Gerät* are like the American apocalyptic quest of Melville in *Moby Dick* in the faster-paced prose of present-day quest novels such as Saul Bellow's *Henderson the Rain King*.

Vonnegut's quick turnabouts of irony and deadpan delivery are as American as Mark Twain, while his works have certain thematic parallels to those of the French Existentialist Albert Camus. His first book *Player Piano,* bears comparison to Huxley's *Brave New World* with its emphasis on human impulses to order and freedom, with the resultant stratification of society and eventual individual rebellion. However, the novels, generally, with their odd mixture of science fiction and realism, are more narrowly American than the works of other American Absurdists.

Barth, though using the American eastern setting and history to great advantage, creating American innocents somewhat in the manner of Washington Irving and James Fenimore Cooper, and adopting William James's Pragmatism as a central viewpoint, also pulls out the stuff of ancient European myth and fable for character and theme, finds aid for his own characters' illogical quests in Musil's *Man Without Qualities,* is fascinated by the ancient frame-tale tradition, particularly in *Scheherazade,* and finds in myth and cyclical narratives an organization for his own quest for meaning within a closed system. He has also profited from reading contemporary European Absurdists, notably Borges, and it is also true that Barth and Beckett have much in common. Beckett's Murphy prefers the "commotion" of the mind to the interpersonal relations of life, and the Unnamable spins endless yarns and is not able to know itself otherwise. The texture of thought in Beckett and Barth is much the same, though Barth's prose expression is much more open, flowing, and bombastic.

The American Absurd, then, is most indigenously American in its Transcendental romantic elements, in its reflection on the idealism of nineteenth-century American values, and in its pragmatic approach to life, both in its subjective pluralism and in its emphasis on balance and a workable relativity. Despite its criticism of our cultural beliefs, it carries a strong moral burden, expressive still of an American belief in personal destiny and the ultimate value of individualism, inner-directedness, and individual conscience. It is not merely an expression of these traits, however, but as we have seen, a viable mode of useful social criticism and artistic experimentation.

Novels such as those of John Irving (for instance, *The World According to Garp*) and Tom Robbins (for instance, *Even Cowgirls Get the Blues*), not to mention the postproletarian black novels of Ishmael Reed (such as, *Flight to Canada*), suggest that the American Absurd is a continuing strain in the contemporary American novel and that so long as we believe in the vitality, possibility, and uniqueness of our nation and of ourselves, our responses to the loss of innocence may well take this form.

Notes

Part I

1. Though he was raised in St. Louis, Mo., and eventually became a British citizen, Eliot's ancestors had lived in New England from 1670 to 1834. Eliot studied at Milton preparatory school in Massachusetts and matriculated at Harvard from 1906 to 1914.
2. *V.* (New York: Random Modern Library, 1963), p. 198.
3. Ibid., p. 412.
4. *The Crying of Lot 49* (New York: Lippincott, 1966), p. 21.
5. See David Cowart, "Pynchon's *The Crying of Lot 49* and the Paintings of Remedios Varo," *Critique* 18, no. 3 (1977). 19-26. For a discussion of the origins of the Trystero and the Thurn and Taxis postal system, see John O. Stark, *Pynchon's Fiction: Thomas Pynchon and the Literature of Information* (Athens, Ohio: Ohio University Press, 1980), p. 108.
6. See David Kirby, "Two Modern Versions of the Quest," *Southern Humanities Review* 5 (Fall 1971), 387-95 and especially 391.
7. Mark Richard Siegel, *Pynchon: Creative Paranoia in Gravity's Rainbow* (New York: Kennikat Press, 1978), p. 60.
8. *Gravity's Rainbow* (New York: Bantam Books, 1973), p. 28.
9. Ibid., p. 237.
10. Ibid., p. 243.
11. Ibid., p. 64.
12 Ibid., p. 266.
13. *V.,* p. 278.
14. *Gravity's Rainbow,* pp. 871-74.
15. Ibid., pp. 62-63.
16. Ibid., p. 831.
17. Ibid., pp. 809-13.
18. Ibid., p. 802.
19. Ibid., p. 718.
20. Ibid., pp. 675-76.

21. Ibid., pp. 194-95.
22. Ibid., p. 28.
23. Ibid., pp. 702-3.
24. Ibid., pp. 850-51.
25. Ibid.
26. For a comparison of *Moby Dick* and *Gravity's Rainbow* see Thomas H. Schaub, *Pynchon: the Voice of Ambiguity* (University of Illinois Press, 1981), pp. 118-120.
27. "The Vault of Language: Self-Reflective Artifice in Contemporary Fiction." *Modern Fiction Studies* 20, no. 3 (Autumn 1974): 350.
28. *Gravity's Rainbow,* pp. 860-61.
29. Ibid., p. 862.
30. Ibid., pp. 594-95.
31. Joseph Fahy has made a case for Pynchon's probable use of Robert Graves's *The White Goddess* in developing the female manifestations of V. See "Thomas Pynchon's *V.* and Mythology," *Critique* 18, no. 3 (1977): 5-18.
32. "Risking the Moment." In *Mindful Pleasures, Essays on Thomas Pynchon,* edited by George Levine and David Leverenz (Boston: Little, Brown, 1976), p. 134.
33. *Gravity's Rainbow,* pp. 548-49.
34. For another view of Pynchon's treatment of Love (leading to entropy), see William Plater, *The Grim Phoenix* (Bloomington: Indiana University Press, 1978), pp. 139-40.
35. In *New World Writing 16,* edited by C. Smith and S. Richardson (New York: Lippincott, 1960), pp. 96, 107-8.
36. *Gravity's Rainbow,* p. 219.
37. *The Great War and Modern Memory* (New York: Oxford U.P., 1975), pp. 332-33.
38. *Gravity's Rainbow,* p. 260.
39. *Kenyon Review,* 22 (Spring 1960): 227, 292.
40. *Gravity's Rainbow,* pp. 744-45.
41. Ibid., pp. 469-70.
42. *V.,* p. 451.
43. *Gravity's Rainbow,* p. 480.
44. Ibid., p. 844.
45. Ibid., p. 541.
46. Ibid., pp. 859-60.
47. Ibid., p. 552.
48. Fussell, pp. 273-77.
49. *V.,* p. 410.
50. *Epoch,* 9 (Spring 1959): 211-13.
51. *V.,* p. 471.

52. Robert E. Golden, "Mass Man and Modern Violence in Pynchon's *V*," *Critique* 14, no. 2 (1927): 15.
53. *V.,* p. 468.
54. *Gravity's Rainbow,* p. 885.
55. Ibid., pp. 814-15.
56. Ibid., p. 865.
57. Ibid., p. 721.
58. Ibid., pp. 727-29.
59. Ibid., p. 351.
60. Pynchon is not the first novelist to see the sex drive and both life and death impulses figured in the firing of a military projectile. On pp. 570-71 of Norman Mailer's *The Naked and the Dead* (New York: Rinehart & Co., Inc., 1948), General Cummings compares the parabolic trajectory of an artillery shell to "the curve of sexual excitement and discharge . . . the curve of the death missile as well as an abstraction of the life-love impulse." Mailer compares the pull of gravity to the "inertia of the masses through which the vision, the upward leap of a culture is blunted, slowed, brought to its early doom."
61. Stephen Heath, *The Nouveau Roman: A Study in the Practice of Writing* (London: Elek Books, 1972), pp. 188-89.
62. "Beyond the Theatre of War: *Gravity's Rainbow,*" *Literature/Film Quarterly* 6 (1978), 347-63.
63. Stark, pp. 22-23.
64. Ibid., p. 82.
65. *From Caligari to Hitler* (Princeton University Press, 1947), p. 150.
66. *Gravity's Rainbow,* pp. 359-65.
67. *The Crying of Lot 49,* p. 138.
68. *Homo Ludens: A Study of the Play Element in Culture* (Boston: Beacon, 1950), p. 2.
69. Fussell, pp. 193-94.
70. *Gravity's Rainbow,* p. 424.
71. *V.,* p. 26.
72. Ibid., pp. 740-43.
73. *Fiction and the Figures of Life* (New York: Knopf, 1970), pp. 191-205.
74. Siegel, p. 37.
76. *Gravity's Rainbow,* pp. 251-53.
77. *V.,* p. 226.
78. Ibid.
79. *Gravity's Rainbow,* p. 334.
80. *V.,* p. 118.
81. *Writing Degree Zero* (New York: Hill and Wang, 1968), p. 30.

Part II

1. *Kurt Vonnegut: The Gospel from Outer Space* (San Bernardino, Calif.: The Borgo Press, 1977), p. 14.
2. *Sirens of Titan* (New York: Dell Publishing Co., 1959), p. 8.
3. Kurt Vonnegut, *Jailbird* (New York: Delacorte Press, 1979), p. xxi.
4. *Vonnegut, A Preface to His Novels* (Port Washington, N.Y.: Kennikat Press, 1977), pp.47-54.
5. *Mother Night* (New York: Avon Books, 1961), p. 124.
6. Ibid., p. 44.
7. Quoted in Stanley Schatt, *Kurt Vonnegut Jr.* (Boston: Twayne Publishers, 1976), p. 52.
8. *Kurt Vonnegut Jr.* (New York: Warner Paperback Library, 1972), p. 109.
9. *God Bless You, Mr. Rosewater* (New York: Dell Publishing Co., 1965), p. 183.
10. Ibid., p. 121.
11. Ibid., p. 56.
12. "Vonnegut's Slaughterhouse-Five and the Fiction of Atrocity," *Critique* 14, no. 3 (1973): 41, 48.
13. Jerome Klinkowitz and John Somer, *The Vonnegut Statement* (New York: Delacorte Press, 1973), p. 118.
14. *Slaughterhouse-Five* (New York: Dell Publishing Co., 1969), p. 117.
15. Kurt Vonnegut (New York: Frederick Ungar Publishing Co., 1977), p. 82.
16. Schatt, pp. 86-87.
17. Quoted in Robert W. Uphaus "Expected Meaning in Vonnegut's Dead-End Fiction," *Novel: A Forum on Fiction* 8, no. 2 (1975): 165.
18. Kurt Vonnegut, Jr. *Wampeters, Foma, and Granfalloons* (New York: Delacorte Press, 1974), pp. xxii-xxiii.
19. *Slaughterhouse-Five*, pp. 188-90.
20. Ibid., p. 101.
21. *Wampeters*, p. 281.
22. *Breakfast of Champions* (New York: Delacorte Press, 1973), p. 221.
23. *Wampeters*, pp. 176-79.
24. *Slapstick* (New York: Delacorte Press, 1976), p. 224.
25. *Slapstick*, pp. 2-3.
26. *Jailbird* (New York: Delacorte Press, 1979, p. x.
27. Ibid., pp. x, xviii-xix.
28. Ibid., p. 236.
29. Ibid., p. 13.
30. Ibid., p. 231.
31. Ibid., p. 235.
32. Ibid., p. 236.
33. Ibid., pp. 25-26.

34. Ibid., p. 63.
35. *The Plague* (New York: Random House Modern Library, 1947), p. 150.
36. "The Myth of Sisyphus." In *Existentialism from Dostoevski to Sartre*, edited by Walter Kaufman (New York: Meridian Books, 1957), p. 313.
37. Ibid., p. 315.
38. Ibid.
39. Lundquist, p. 86.
40. "Kurt Vonnegut as Science-Fiction Writer." In *Vonnegut in America*, edited by Jerome Klinkowitz and Donald Lawler (New York: Delacorte Press, 1977), p. 93.
41. Lundquist, p. 10.
42. *Slaughterhouse-Five*, p. 125.
43. Schatt, p. 149.
44. "The Modes of Vonnegut's Fiction." In *The Vonnegut Statement*, p. 202.
45. Schatt, p. 150.
46. Klinkowitz, *Vonnegut in America*, p. 23.
47. Lundquist, pp. 14-15.
48. *Wampeters*, pp. 214-15.
49. Introduction to *Three Soldiers* (New York: Random House Modern Library, 1932), pp. vii-viii.
50. "Vonnegut's Satire." In *Vonnegut in America*, pp. 133-49.
51. "The Divine Stupidity of Kurt Vonnegut," *Esquire* (Sept. 1970): 196.
52. *Happy Birthday, Wanda June* (New York: Delacorte Press, 1971), p. ix.
53. Ibid., p. 52.
54. *Breakfast of Champions*, p. 210.
55. Klinkowitz, *Vonnegut in America*, p. 17.
56. "*Cat's Cradle* and Traditional American Humor," *Journal of Popular Culture* 5 (1972): 958.
57. *Wampeters*, p. 262.
58. Quoted in Leverence, p. 962.
59. *Jailbird*, pp. xv-xvi.
60. "Technique as Recovery: *Lolita* and *Mother Night*." In *Vonnegut in America*, pp. 97-133.
61. Ibid., p. 119.
62. *Kurt Vonnegut, Fantasist of Fire and Ice* (Bowling Green University Popular Press, 1972), 40-41.
63. Lundquist, p. 69.
64. Schatt, pp. 83-84.
65. *Wampeters*, pp. xxvi-xxvii.
66. See Schatt, p. 116.
67. Vonnegut has often acknowledged a deep respect for the work, humor, and ironic attitude toward life of Mark Twain. A lengthy statement in praise of Twain occurs in Vonnegut's recently published miscellany *Palm Sunday*

(New York: Delacorte Press, 1981), pp. 166-72.

Part III

1. *Lost in the Funhouse* (New York: Doubleday, 1968), pp. 4-6.
2. Ibid., p. 103.
3. *The Floating Opera,* rev. ed. (Garden City, N.Y.: Doubleday, 1967), pp. 168-69.
4. Ibid., p. 218.
5. Ibid., p. 51.
6. Ibid., p. 22.
7. Ibid., p. 223.
8. "Todd Andrews, Ontological Insecurity, and the Floating Opera," *Critique* 18, no 2 (1977): 34-49.
9. *The Floating Opera,* p. 250.
10. Ibid., p. 252.
11. Ibid., p. 6.
12. *John Barth; an Introduction* (The Pennsylvania State University Press, 1976), p. 16.
13. *Robert Musil, Master of the Hovering Life* (New York: Columbia University Press, 1978), pp. 195-96.
14. David S. Luft, *Robert Musil and the Crisis of European Culture 1880-1942* (Berkeley: University of California Press, 1980), p. 116.
15. *End of the Road,* rev. ed. (Garden City, N.Y.: Doubleday, 1967), pp. 112-13.
16. Ibid., p. 76.
17. Ibid., p. 122.
18. Ibid., p. 85.
19. Ibid., p. 44.
20. Morrell, p. 33.
21. "*The Sot-Weed Factor:* a Contemporary Mock Epic," *Critique* 8, 2 (1966): 88.
22. "The Historical Ebeneezer Cooke," *Critique* 10, no. 3 (1968): 53.
23. "The Use and Abuse of Smith's *Generall Historie* in John Barth's *The Sot-Weed Factor,*" 2 (1975), pp. 105-15.
24. *The Literature of Exhaustion* (Durham, N.C.: Duke University Press, 1974), p. 131.
25. *The Sot-Weed Factor,* rev. ed. (New York: Bantam Books, Inc., 1967), p. 12.
26. Ibid., p. 66.
27. Ibid., p. 537.
28. Ibid., p. 373.
29. Ibid., p. 529.

30. Ibid., pp. 138-39.
31. Ibid., p. 458.
32. *Black Humor Fiction of the Sixties* (Athens, Ohio: Ohio University Press, 1973), p. 7.
33. *The End of the Road,* p. 130.
34. See Morrell, pp. 56, 126-27. In 1953, Barth began a set of tales set in Maryland's Dorchester County. Many of these were incorporated in *The Sot-Weed Factor,* accounting, in part, for its interpolated tales and fragmentary qualities. Morrell counts twenty-five separate stories within the body of the novel. There are poetry, sections of diaries, recipes, and other bits and pieces as well.
35. Morrell, pp. 60-64.
   Raymond Olderman, *Beyond the Waste Land: A Study of the American Novel in the 1960's* (New Haven: Yale University Press, 1972), p. 81.
   Jac Thorpe, *John Barth; the Comic Sublimity of* (Carbondale, Ill.: Southern Illinois University Press, 1974), pp. 56-57.
36. *Giles Goat-Boy, or The Revised New Syllabus* (Greenwich, Conn.: Fawcett Publications, Inc., 1966), p. 353.
37. Ibid., pp. 524-25.
38. Ibid., p. 404.
39. Ibid., p. 748.
40. See Thrope, pp. 66-67. See also James T. Gresham, *"Giles Goat-Boy:* Satyr, Satire, Tragedy Twined," *Genre* 7 (1974): 150-57.
41. *Giles Goat-Boy,* p. 63.
42. Ibid., pp. 464-65.
43. Ibid., p. 505.
44. Ibid., p. 456.
45. Ibid., p. 618.
46. Annie Le Rebellier, "A Spectatorial Skeptic: An Interview with John Barth," *Caliban* 12 (1975): 107.
47. *Giles Goat-Boy,* pp. 732-35.
48. Ibid., pp. 240-45.
49. Ibid., p. 746.
50. Ibid., p. 672.
51. Ibid., pp. 415-17, 492-95.
52. Ibid., p. 740.
53. Ibid., pp. 733-35.
54. Ibid., p. 709.
55. Ibid., p. 731.
56. Ibid., pp. 734-35.
57. Quoted in Morrell, p. 77.
58. *Giles Goat-Boy,* p. 354.
59. Ibid., p. 425.

60. Ibid., p. 759.
61. Ibid., p. 755.
62. Ibid., pp. xvii-xviii.
63. Olderman, p. 88.
64. Thorpe, p. 10.
65. Quoted in Morrell, p. 69.
66. Schulz, p. 31.
67. "The Anti-Novels of John Barth," *Chicago Review* 20, no. 3 (1968): 101.
68. Morrell, p. 140.
69. *The Atlantic* 220 (Aug. 1967): 34.
70. *The End of the Road,* p. 4.
71. Stark, p. 121.
72. Barth quoted in Morrell, p. 124.
73. For a different interpretation of the Moebius strip symbolism see Victor J. Vitanza, "The Novelist as Topologist: John Barth's *Lost in the Funhouse, Texas Studies in Literature and Language* 19 (1977): 84.
74. "The Literature of Exhaustion," p. 33.
75. *Chimera* (New York: Random, 1972), p. 10.
76. Morrell, pp. 162-632.
77. *Chimera,* p. 11.
78. Ibid., pp. 53-56.
79. Morrell, pp. 142-43.
80. Ibid., pp. 144-45.
81. Jerry Powell, "John Barth's *Chimera*: a Creative Response to the Literature of Exhaustion," *Critique* 18, no. 2 (1977): 63.
82. *Chimera,* p. 142.
83. Ibid., pp. 303-4.
84. *Letters* (New York: Putnam, 1979), pp. 88-89.
85. Ibid., p. 88.
86. Ibid., p. 17.
87. Ibid., pp. 278, 706.
88. Ibid., p. 730.
89. Ibid., pp. 734, 738.
90. Ibid., pp. 742-45.
91. Ibid., p. 324.
92. Ibid., p. 636.
93. Ibid., p. 641.
94. Ibid., p. 329.
95. Ibid., p. 368.
96. Ibid., p. 393.
97. Ibid.,p. 163.
98. Ibid., p. 348.
99. Ibid., pp. 384-85, 38-41.

100. Ibid., p. 332.
101. Ibid., pp. 650-51.
102. Ibid., p. 367.
103. Ibid., pp. 766-68.
104. "A Novel of Correspondences," *New York Times Book Review,* Sept. 30, 1979, p. 33.
105. "The Lives of His Mind," *Saturday Review* (Oct. 13, 1979): 73.
106. *The New Republic* (Dec. 1, 1979): 37.
107. *Atlantic* 245 (Jan. 1980): 70.
108. (New York: Putnam, 1982).
109. "An Interview with John Barth," *Contemporary Literature* 22, no. 1 (1981): 7.

Index

Adamov, Arthur, 2
Adams, Henry, 9, 10, 19-20
Aesop, 70
Barth, John, 4, 36, 77-113, 117-122, 129; *Chimera,* 101-103, 110-111, "Bellerophoniad," 103, "Dunyazadiad," 102, "Perseid," 102-103, 110; *The End of the Road,* 82-85, 88, 101, 105-106, 109, 110, 121; *The Floating Opera,* 79-83, 104-106; *Giles Goat-Boy,* 91-101, 103, 104, 108, 118, 120; *LETTERS,* 101-113, 120; *Lost In the Funhouse:* "Anonymiad," 78-79, 80, "Echo," 77, "Lost In the Funhouse," 77-78, 101, "Menelaiad," 81, 101, "Night Sea Journey," 78, 85, "Title," 112; *Sabbatical,* 112-113; *The Sot-Weed Factor,* 85-89, 104, 106, 119, 129
Barthes, Roland, 32, 39, 121
Beckett, Samuel, 1, 2, 38, 122
Bellow, Saul, 36, 73, 80, 121
Bergson, Henri, 10, 18, 99
Borges, Jorge Luis, 37, 99, 101, 112
Bradbury, Ray, 66
Brautigan, Richard, 4
Brooks, Van Wyck, 60
Bunyan, John, 72
Burroughs, William, 48, 56
Calvino, Italo, 111

Campbell, Joseph, 91
Camus, Albert, 1, 61-62, 71, 79, 121
Céline, Louis-Ferdinand, 52, 53
Coleridge, Samuel Taylor, 34
Cooke, Ebeneezer, 86
Cooper, James Fenimore, 89, 121
Coover, Robert, 4
Descartes, René, 118
Dillinger, John, 28, 58
Darwin, Charles, 18
Dickens, Charles, 71
Disney, Walt, 36
Dostoevski, Feodor, 49, 55, 82
Durrenmatt, Friedrich, 1
Edwards, Jonathan, 9, 19
Eliot, John, 71
Eliot, Thomas Stearns, 9, 20-21, 72, 77, 98, 123
Ellison, Ralph, 36
Emerson, Ralph Waldo, 9, 18, 19, 34, 86, 97
Existentialism, 1, 2, 85, 119. *See* Camus, Hemingway, and Sartre
Farben, I.G., 14, 59
Fielding, Henry, 85
Fitzgerald, F. Scott, 10, 38, 59, 64, 112
Frazer, James, 28
Freud, Sigmund, 20, 24, 25
Gass, W., 37
Hapgood, Powers, 58